ALEF-TAV's
HEBREW LIVING™ LETTERS

24 WISDOMS
DEEPER KINGDOM BIBLE STUDY

First Edition.

Published by:
Sapphire Throne Ministries
Masonville, Colorado
sapphirethroneministries.com
sapphirethroneministries@gmail.com

Managing Editor: Robin Shukle
Design: Liz Mrofka
whatifpublishing.com

Cover Image: Robin Main

Printed by: Kindle Direct Publishing

ISBN: 978-0-9985982-6-0

ALEF-TAV's
HEBREW LIVING™ LETTERS

————— ∞ —————

24 WISDOMS
DEEPER KINGDOM BIBLE STUDY

ROBIN MAIN

TABLE OF CONTENTS

BE STILL AND KNOW

The Lover of our souls meets us in the Word whose pages are His flesh. As we lay our head on His reassuring chest, we fall in love with the Word of God again and again and again. Faith comes by hearing His heartbeat, and hearing by God's anointed utterance of the Anointed One (Rom. 10:17). Listen to the Messiah's heartbeat in conjunction with His incredible Word, which creates such a deep longing. *"Deep calls to deep"* (Psa. 42:7). May the LORD God Almighty awaken your innermost being, as you long for more of Him. Come. Let's get carried away, as we walk arm-in-arm into the light of ALEF-TAV (את).

Yeshua (i.e., Jesus) is ALEF-TAV (את) and He is the Word of God (Rev. 19:13). May you encounter our magnificent Messiah in a whole new light through focusing on the Lord of Love's exquisite golden belt of truth to be taken into His glorious garden with the Tree of Life in its midst. Everything in Creation has been made to help us see and understand the Creator because His extravagant love for us inspired it all. The sword of the Cherubim that guards the way to the Tree of Life is the Word of God (Gen. 3:24). When you concentrate your affections upon the Lover of your soul, not only do you gain access to the Tree of Life (which is Him) but you also encounter the wondrous Water of Life. Listen to our Beloved's beautiful heart: " *¹² My darling bride, my private paradise. Fastened to My heart. A secret spring that no one else can have are you—my bubbling fountain hidden from public view. What a perfect partner to Me now that I have you. ¹³⁻¹⁴ Your inward life is now sprouting, bringing forth fruit. What a beautiful paradise unfolds within you . . . ¹⁵ You are a fountain of gardens. A well of living water springs up from within you, like a mountain brook flowing into My heart"* (Song of Songs 8:12-15 ₜₚₜ).

Within are the seeds of opportunity and growth for those who desire to dive deeper into the Word of God and His Kingdom. The divine secrets, revelation, and strategies for the days ahead demand that we go deeper. The enclosed revelatory information and questions at the end of each chapter will challenge and enlighten you, as you rise to the occasion.

Many have told me that they don't know how to go into the depths of God's Word. This *ALEF-TAV's Hebrew Living™ Letters* Deeper Kingdom Bible Study will teach you through hands-on experience. Before you start, it is wise to pray for a spirit of wisdom and revelation in the knowledge of Him (Eph. 1:17). Prayerfully studying Scripture the way this book leads will add splendid layers upon layers to your wisdom, understanding, and knowledge. The more you dive into the depths of Scripture, the more you can pull from. The deeper your foundation in the Word, the higher you can fly by the Holy Spirit. This is one of the keys to worshiping the Father in Spirit and in Truth (John 4:24).

Not only is it wisdom to pray before studying God's Word, but choosing to lay down any preconceived notions and paradigms to let the Word interpret itself is key to truly knowing the heart and mind of Almighty God. All Scriptures are in bold italics. When you see bold italics, it's ALEF-TAV (את)—the Word of God—personally speaking to you.

Even though this ALEF-TAV Bible Study goes into wonderful depths, it is not all-inclusive. For instance, not all the references to "house" or "dwelling place" are listed. You will have to mine those magnificent riches yourself. That being said, this Deeper Kingdom Bible Study will give you a tremendous start. Unless otherwise specified, the Biblical translation used is the New King James Version (NKJV).

I call the enclosed 24 ALEF-TAV Bible Studies the "24 Wisdoms" because the Lord gives wisdom to those who incline their ears and understanding to those who apply their hearts (Prov. 2:2). Wisdom is for those who treasure God's Word. Proverbs 4:7 tells us that wisdom is the principal thing; therefore, get wisdom and with it understanding. When wisdom is exalted in your own life, Scripture says she will promote you (Prov. 4:8). In other words, you will grow in the way of wisdom. That's why the questions and contemplations at the end of each Deeper Kingdom Bible Study section, which features either ALEF-TAV (את) or one of the Hebrew letters, are called "The Way of Wisdom."

After "The Way of Wisdom" interactive section, there is a page where you are invited to meditate more on what you have learned. Then, you can practice drawing a letter of the Hebrew Alphabet. You might want to use a calligraphy pen, and you are encouraged to do as the Hebrews do—write from right to left. The calligraphy pages are printed with black on the back to help absorb the ink. You may also consider sliding a thick piece of paper or a thin piece of cardboard between the pages for added protection. Please continue to be purposely meditative about what you just learned as you practice writing a particular Hebrew letter. I would suggest that you jot down what comes to mind. After you practice writing a letter of the Hebrew Alphabet, there is a final honey highlight for each Hebrew letter. This concluding whisper from God reveals a little more about each Hebrew letter, demonstrating their endless nature. It also ties the concepts in this Deeper Kingdom Bible Study to *Sapphire Throne Ministries'* more advanced book about the Hebrew letters—*Quantum 22*™. You are encouraged to taste and see these sweet facets of ALEF-TAV's wraparound presence.

Throughout the ALEF-TAV Bible Study, there are blank sections entitled "Thoughts." This is to create space to listen and to be heard. It is also meant to make room within you to discover the energy and character of each Hebrew letter. To assist in this endeavor, the last page of this Bible Study is about keeping track of your "Reflections." It can serve as a super list to help keep track of what is most important to you as well as serving as a place to collect the revelations you'd like to remember. In your journey to learn about ALEF-TAV (את) and His Hebrew letters, be free to go where the Holy Spirit guides. You can also linger longer to experience more of His goodness.

You are encouraged to make this book your own. You can either make notes in the margins of this book, or you might want to start a separate notebook where you write down your thoughts. We have created a commonplace book—*Dwelling in the Presence of the Divine: A Commonplace Book of the Hebrew Living*™ *Letters*—that is made to help you collect your thoughts on a topic (e.g., the first Hebrew letter ALEF (א)). It's simply another way to assist you being mindful and present with the Most High God. When I study this way, I usually draw a picture or two as I focus on the Way and the Truth and the Life. The Lord has shown me that this meditative writing and drawing practice, as you focus on Christ, grows a "knowing" gift within you about His will and His ways. It is my hope that people take what is taught in this book and apply the principles to their own walk. The ALEF-TAV

Deeper Kingdom Bible Study will be gloriously different for each person because we are each unique. Additionally, our past, present, and future effects how we see, perceive, and understand.

You will notice I mainly call Jesus "Yeshua" in this book. Yeshua is the Aramaic/Hebrew name for "Jesus." It was the name He was called when He walked the earth. It's a shortened form of Yehoshua, which means "salvation" or "the Lord saves." While Jesus has asked me to call Him Yeshua, I don't believe others are required to do the same. Please be led of the Lord.

Everyone is encouraged to not get hung up on gender stuff. Know that "in Christ" there is no gender in the Spirit. We are all one in the Messiah: *"There is neither Jew nor Greek, there is neither slave nor free, there is neither male nor female; for you are all one in Christ Jesus" (Galatians 3:28).* When the pronouns of he or she are referenced within, it's about function. Know that men are part of the Bride of Christ and women are part of the sons of God.

Everyone is also urged to test everything contained within this Deeper Kingdom Bible Study with Scripture and the Spirit of the Living God. Do not rely on what man says. Rely on God and test the spirits (1 John 4:1-4). You will find several controversial topics, such as the Star of David, Melchizedek, and Metatron. Know that I have done my due diligence in testing these matters. For instance, I kept hearing that the Star of David (sometimes called Solomon's Seal or the Merkabah) was demonic due to its use in many cultures and religions. So, I laid down what I and others thought and asked Yeshua if the Star of David was good and of Him. I continually sought Him for months before I got His answer. Messiah Yeshua told me that the Star of David was of Him; and it is good, godly, and righteous in its original and redeemed state. The enemy has to use what God has created. Just because Satanists and others may use something in a demonic way doesn't mean that it isn't of Him. It is similar when someone poisons food, it doesn't mean all food is corrupt and poisonous. So it is with the Star of David, Melchizedek, Metatron, etc. Each of these have a twisted counterpart to a righteous reality. Know that if something has a righteous root, it will be redeemed to its pristine state. If its root is demonic, Messiah Yeshua and the people who are one with Him will judge it according to His perfect heart and do away with it. This is part of the restoration of all things.

It will be extremely beneficial to have additional resources on hand, like dictionaries, encyclopedias, concordances, etc. An online resource that I highly recommend is the *Blue Letter Bible* (https://www.blueletterbible.org/), especially their *Strong's Concordance* references for each verse. Another excellent online resource is *Bible Gateway* (https://www.biblegateway.com/) with its many versions of the Bible and excellent search capabilities. If you desire to delve more into the Hebrew aspects of Scripture, you might enjoy *Sefaria* (https://www.sefaria.org/).

Please enjoy flowing by the vibrant and wise Holy Spirit, as you look to ALEF-TAV (את)—the Author and Perfecter of your faith.

BLESSED

is the one who connects to
ALEF-TAV (את)—
the Maker of heaven and earth.

ALEF-TAV

WISDOM ONE

את
ALEF-TAV

ALEF-TAV (את)

Messiah Yeshua (i.e., Jesus Christ) has many names. One is the Word of God and another is ALEF-TAV (את), which is commonly translated as "the First and the Last" or "the Alpha and the Omega":

> "*¹ The Revelation of Jesus Christ, which God gave Him to show to His bond-servants, the things which must soon take place; and He sent and communicated it by His angel to His bond-servant John, ² who testified to the <u>Word of God</u> and to the <u>testimony of Jesus Christ</u>, everything that he saw. ³ Blessed is the one who reads, and those who hear the words of the prophecy and keep the things which are written in it; for the time is near. . . . ⁸ '<u>I am the Alpha [ALEF] and the Omega [TAV]</u>,' says the Lord God, 'who is and who was and who is to come, the Almighty.' . . . ¹⁷ When I saw Him, I fell at His feet like a dead man. And He placed His right hand on me, saying, 'Do not be afraid; <u>I am the first [ALEF] and the last [TAV]</u>, ¹⁸ and the living One; and I was dead, and behold, I am alive forevermore, and I have the keys of death and of Hades' " (Revelation 1:1-3, 8, 17-18 Additions mine).*

> "*¹¹ And I saw heaven opened, and behold, a white horse, and He who sat on it is called Faithful and True, and in righteousness He judges and wages war. ¹² His eyes are a flame of fire, and on His head are many crowns; and He has a name written on Him which no one knows except Himself. ¹³ He is clothed with a robe dipped in blood, and <u>His name is called The Word of God</u>. ¹⁴ And the armies which are in heaven, clothed in fine linen, white and clean, were following Him on white horses. ¹⁵ From His mouth comes a sharp sword, so that with it He may strike down the nations, and He will rule them with a rod of iron; and He treads the wine press of the fierce wrath of God, the Almighty. ¹⁶ And on His robe and on His thigh He has a name written: 'KING OF KINGS, AND LORD OF LORDS' " (Revelation 19:11-16 NASB).*

> "*¹² Behold, I am coming quickly, and My reward is with Me, to reward each one as his work deserves. ¹³ <u>I am the Alpha [ALEF] and the Omega [TAV], the first and the last, the beginning and the end</u>." ¹⁴ Blessed are those who wash their robes, so that they will have the right to the Tree of Life, and may enter the city by the gates. ¹⁵ Outside are the dogs, the sorcerers, the sexually immoral persons, the murderers, the idolaters, and everyone who loves and practices lying. ¹⁶ 'I, Jesus, have sent My angel to testify to you of these things*

for the churches. I am the root and the descendant of David, the bright morning star.'
¹⁷ The Spirit and the bride say, 'Come.' And let the one who hears say, 'Come.' And let
the one who is thirsty come; let the one who desires, take the water of life without cost"
*(Revelation 22:12-17*_{NASB Additions mine}*).*

"Let there be light" is the first declaration of God's will in Scripture, but He could not have spoken it without first creating a language to communicate His thoughts. *"Then God said, 'Let there be light'; and there was light. And God saw the light, that it was good; and God divided the light from the darkness" (Genesis 1:3-4).*

Humans voice their thoughts through a language, with letters being a language's building blocks. They are simply emulating how the Lord spoke in the beginning. Before God could speak the universe into existence, He had to first create the language to speak forth His will. *"You are worthy, O Lord, To receive glory and honor and power; For You created all things, And by Your will they exist and were created" (Revelation 4:11).* A fundamental concept for Hebrew Sages is that the letters of the Hebrew Alef-Bet were created first of all out of nothing but God's desire—His divine will. They say, "By use of the letters, the Holy One, Blessed is He, created all the worlds."

There is a hidden meaning behind the first verse in the Bible. In English, we read: *"In the beginning God created the heavens and the earth."* However, in Hebrew, it says: *"Bereshit barà Elohim et hashamaim veet haaretz."* After the words *"In the beginning God created" (Bereshit barà Elohim)* and before the word *"heaven" (hashamaim)*, there is the word *et*. Notice that is seven Hebrew words, but only six get translated. The untranslated word *et* is composed of the Hebrew letters ALEF (א) and TAV (ת), which are the first and last letters of the Hebrew Alef-Bet. This is one of the reasons why the Hebrew sages say that God created the Hebrew Alphabet first; and then, He used them to create heaven and earth.

Throughout Scripture, there are random references to ALEF-TAV (את) that have been largely disregarded when Jews read their Bible, or when Scripture has been translated into other languages, including English. So far it seems that mainly Jewish Mystics have tried to delve into the reason why those random ALEF-TAVs exist in the written word.

Perhaps these scholars have overlooked the Messianic reference: *"Thus says the* LORD*, the King of Israel and His Redeemer, the* LORD *of hosts: I am the first [ALEF] and I am the last [TAV], and there is no God besides Me." (Isaiah 44:6*_{Additions mine}*)* Fundamentally, we need to remember that Messiah Yeshua declares in Revelation 1:8, *"I am the Alpha and the Omega . . . who is and who was and who is to come, the Almighty."* Yeshua is the ALEF-TAV or as He says, I AM the ALEF-TAV, and there is no God besides Me.

Not only is Messiah Yeshua the Beginning and End of all creation, He is also the Creator and Sustainer of all things: *"For by Him were all things created that are in heaven, and that are in earth, visible and invisible, whether they be thrones, or dominions, or principalities, or powers: all things were created by Him and for Him: And He is before all things and by Him all things consist" (Colossians 1:16-17).*

Thoughts

When Messiah Yeshua testifies that He is the ALEF and the TAV (את), He is making several connections:

- *"Who has performed and done it, Calling the generations from the beginning? 'I, the Lord, am the first [ALEF]; And with the last [TAV] I am He'" (Isaiah 41:4 _{Additions mine}).*

- *"Thus says the Lord, the King of Israel, And His Redeemer, the Lord of hosts: 'I am the First [ALEF] and I am the Last [TAV]; Besides Me there is no God" (Isaiah 44:6 _{Additions mine}).*

- *"Listen to Me, O Jacob, And Israel, My called: I am He, I am the First [ALEF], I am also the Last [TAV]. ¹³ Indeed My hand has laid the foundation of the earth, And My right hand has stretched out the heavens; When I call to them, They stand up together" (Isaiah 48:12-13 _{Additions mine}).*

- *"I am the Alpha [ALEF] and the Omega [TAV], the Beginning [rosh] and the End [sof], the First [rishon] and the Last [acharon]" (Revelation 22:13 _{Additions mine}).*

The spiritual realm, where the Almighty dwells, is composed of perfect thoughts and pure concepts—not needing to be clothed in words and letters. Think of telepathic communication. When our Heavenly Father, Messiah Yeshua, and the Holy Spirit created the Hebrew Alphabet out of the Messiah's essence, God ordered spiritual forces of creation through its twenty-two sacred Hebrew letters before there was even one other act of creation.

The existence of everything created from people to poodles to puddles depends upon the spiritual content with which it was created. By uttering the famous *"Let there be"* words, we can say that the Word—ALEF-TAV (את)—created all of what can be classified as Creation (Col. 1:15-17).

It is an incredible mystery how Yeshua *"existed before all things"* and is *"the first born of all creation"* at the same time. When one understands that the array of individual spiritual forces ordered via the Hebrew Alphabet was resident in Yeshua before those letters or that language was created, one can get a glimpse into the vast mystery of Yeshua being the firstborn of all creation.

"In the beginning was the Word, and the Word was with God, and the Word was God" (John 1:1). The Word is made up of letters. *"In the beginning God created ALEF-TAV" (Genesis 1:1).* The Hebrew Living™ Letters— these individual spiritual forces—inherent in Christ was birthed from His essential, intrinsic essence, which was originally included wholly in the Word. The firstborn of all creation is the very thing that constitutes every living substance. It is the protoplasm of the universe.

It is the individual spiritual forces that originally belonged, and still belong, to the nature of Christ. The firstborn of all creation is the letters of the Word—the Hebrew Alphabet. Basically, Messiah Yeshua's spoken words marshaled spiritual forces that facilitated Creation according to His divine will. Like some sort of excellent, exalted scientist, Yeshua "spoke" the perfect blend of spiritual forces that produced light (Genesis 1:3). Another blend produced heaven and all its fullness (Genesis 1:6) Yet another blend produced vegetation yielding seed (Genesis 1:11), and so on and so forth ad infinitum.

Thoughts

The following is the list of the *Hebrew Living™ Letters*, which are the firstborn of all creation birthed from the Word of God:

Letter	Pronunciation	Picture	Ordinal Value	Numerical Value
א - Alef	ah-lef	ox, bull	1	1
ב/בּ - Bet/Vet	bet or bayt	tent, house	2	2
ג - Gimel	geeh-mel	camel	3	3
ד - Dalet	dah-let	door	4	4
ה - Hei	hey	behold	5	5
ו/וֹ - Vav/Waw	vahv	nail, peg	6	6
ז - Zayin	ZAH-yeen	sword, weapon	7	7
ח - Chet	rhymes with "met," sound of "ch" as in Bach	fence, inner room	8	8
ט - Tet	rhymes with "mate," sound of "t" as in tall	snake, coiling	9	9
י - Yud	yood, rhymes with "mode"	hand (closed)	10	10
כ/ך - Kaf/Khaf	kaf with sound of "k" as in kite	palm (open hand)	11	20
ל - Lamed	lah-med	rod or staff	12	30
מ - Mem	mem with sound of "m" as in mom	water	13	40
נ - Nun	noon	fish	14	50
ס - Samech	sah-mekh	prop	15	60
ע - Ayin	ah-yeen	eye	16	70
פ/פּ - Pey/Fey	pay	mouth	17	80
צ - Tsadek	tsah-dek	fishhook	18	90
ק - Koof	kof with sound of "q" as in queen	back of the head	19	100
ר - Resh	raysh	head	20	200
שׁ/שׂ - Shin/Sin	sheen	tooth	21	300
ת - Tav	tav	sign (cross)	22	400

With the words, *"Let there be"* creation came into existence in our spacetime continuum at that primeval instant. The words that brought creation into being remain within them and with us every instant. He *"upholds all things by the word of His power"* (Hebrews 1:3). Everything continues to exist because not an instant goes by without God continuing to voice, in effect, *"Let there be"* in the sense that the Divine will of the original six days remain in force.

Yeshua is the Word. Yeshua is the mysterious ALEF-TAV (את). When we consider that not only is Messiah Yeshua the Beginning and the End but also the Creator and Sustainer of all things, we can understand that *et* (ALEF-TAV) includes all the various objects of creation within heaven and earth. This all began when Yeshua's infinite light filled the void—empty space—which is our entire created reality.

Thoughts

The Way Of Wisdom

1. Why does Messiah Yeshua conceal His mysterious name ALEF-TAV (את)?
   Hint: Meditate on Proverbs 25:2.

   _____

   _____

   _____

2. What's the personal significance to you that Messiah Yeshua declares Himself to be the ALEF (א) and the TAV (ת)?

   _____

   _____

   _____

3. What's the implication of the hidden ALEF-TAV (את) being mentioned in the first verse of the Bible (Genesis 1:1)?

   _____

   _____

   _____

4. Three verses in the Book of Isaiah contain "the first" and "the last" (Isa. 41:4, Isa. 44:6, Isa. 48:12). When you read these verses, what is the Holy Spirit highlighting to you and why? Be sure to read these verses in context (i.e., Read the verses around them, possibly the entire chapter.)

   _____

   _____

   _____

5. Make note of the other names associated with God that are attached to the disclosure of ALEF-TAV (את); then check in with the Lord as you contemplate why they are linked together.

   The Almighty (Rev. 1:8): _____

   _____

   _____

   _____

The Living One (Rev. 1:18): _____

_____

_____

_____

Faithful and True (Rev. 19:11): _____

_____

_____

_____

The Word of God (Rev. 19:13): _____

_____

_____

_____

King of Kings and Lord of Lords (Rev. 19:16): _____

_____

_____

_____

The Beginning and The End (Rev. 22:13): _____

_____

_____

_____

The Root and The Descendant of David (Rev. 22:16): _____

_____

_____

_____

The Bright Morning Star (Rev. 22:16): _____

_____

_____

_____

NOT-SO-RANDOM
ALEF-TAVS

WISDOM TWO

את

NOT-SO-RANDOM
ALEF-TAVS

We have seen that the first ALEF-TAV (את) occurs in Genesis 1:1. *"In the beginning God created the heavens and the earth (Bereshit barà Elohim **et (את)** hashamaim veet haaretz)."* Other not-so-random ALEF-TAV (את)s are found throughout Scripture. Notice the Messianic flavor of the ALEF-TAV references in Micah 5:1 and Zechariah 12:10.

Micah 5:1-2 prophetically speaks of the Messiah being born in Bethlehem and being struck with a rod on the cheek. Messiah Yeshua (Jesus Christ) fulfilled both of these. The latter was fulfilled just before His crucifixion: *"¹ Now gather yourself in troops, O daughter of troops; He has laid siege against us; They will strike [**ALEF-TAV (את)**] the judge of Israel with a rod on the cheek. ² "But you, Bethlehem Ephrathah, Though you are little among the thousands of Judah, Yet out of you shall come forth to Me The One to be Ruler in Israel, Whose goings forth are from of old, From everlasting" (Micah 5:1-2 _{Additions mine}).*

The Hebrew translation of these two verses goes like this:

(עַתָּה תִּתְגֹּדְדִי בַת־גְּדוּד מָצוֹר שָׂם עָלֵינוּ בַּשֵּׁבֶט יַכּוּ עַל־הַלְּחִי **אֵת** שֹׁפֵט יִשְׂרָאֵל)

"Now you gash yourself in grief.
They have laid siege to us;
They strike the **ALEF-TAV (את)** ruler of Israel
On the cheek with a staff.

(וְאַתָּה בֵּית־לֶחֶם אֶפְרָתָה צָעִיר לִהְיוֹת בְּאַלְפֵי יְהוּדָה מִמְּךָ לִי יֵצֵא לִהְיוֹת מוֹשֵׁל בְּיִשְׂרָאֵל וּמוֹצָאֹתָיו מִקֶּדֶם מִימֵי עוֹלָם:)

And you, O Bethlehem of Ephrath,
Least among the clans of Judah,
From you one shall come forth
To rule Israel for Me—
One whose origin is from of old,
From ancient times."[1]

---

[1]Micah 4:14; Micah 5:1. JPS, 1985. https://www.sefaria.org/Micah.4.14 and https://www.sefaria.org/Micah.5.1. Note that the verses are numbered differently in the Hebrew version versus the NKJV English translation.

Zechariah 12:10 also prophetically speaks of the Messiah being pierced, which literally happened when Yeshua was nailed to the Cross.

> *"And I will pour out on the house of David and on the inhabitants of Jerusalem the Spirit of grace and of pleading, so that they will look at Me [ALEF-TAV (את)] whom they pierced; and they will mourn for Him, like one mourning for an only son, and they will weep bitterly over Him like the bitter weeping over a firstborn"* (Zechariah 12:10 NASB Additions mine). **This is confirmed in the Book of Isaiah in the 53rd chapter:** *"But He was pierced for our offenses, He was crushed for our wrongdoings; The punishment for our well-being was laid upon Him, And by His wounds we are healed"* (Isaiah 53:5 NASB).

The Hebrew translation of Zechariah 12:10 goes like this:

וְשָׁפַכְתִּי עַל־בֵּית דָּוִיד וְעַל ׀ יוֹשֵׁב יְרוּשָׁלַ͏ִם רוּחַ חֵן וְתַחֲנוּנִים וְהִבִּיטוּ אֵלַי אֵת אֲשֶׁר־דָּקָרוּ וְסָפְדוּ עָלָיו כְּמִסְפֵּד עַל־הַיָּחִיד וְהָמֵר עָלָיו כְּהָמֵר עַל־הַבְּכוֹ

But I will fill the House of David and the inhabitants of Jerusalem with a spirit of pity and compassion; and they shall lament to Me about those who are slain, wailing over them as over a favorite son and showing bitter grief as over a first-born.

As you can see, ALEF-TAV (את) is a profound mystery. Probably the first mystic ever was the Creator Himself; because the word "mystic" comes from the Latin *mysticus*, which means "of mysteries." The Word of God has at least twenty-one references to the terms "mystery" and "mysteries." Here are a few of my favorites:

- **It's been given to Christ's disciples to know the <u>mysteries</u> of the Kingdom of Heaven (Matthew 13:11), and <u>mysteries</u> of the Kingdom of God (Luke 8:10).**

- **God's people are called stewards of the <u>mysteries</u> of God (1 Corinthians 4:1).**

- **We are to make manifest the <u>mystery of Christ</u> in word and deed (Colossians 4:3).**

- **We speak the wisdom of God by the Spirit of God in a <u>mystery</u> among them that are perfect (1 Corinthians 2:7).**

- **There is the fellowship of the <u>mystery</u> between Messiah Yeshua and His Church according to the eternal purposes in Christ Jesus (Ephesians 3:9).**

- **There is a great <u>mystery</u> concerning Christ and the Church being one flesh . . . of Christ loving the church so much that He gave Himself for it to sanctify and cleanse it with the washing of the water of the word (Ephesians 5:26).**

- **We are to hold onto the <u>mystery</u> of faith to be proven and found blameless (1 Timothy 3:9).**

Whenever the term "mystic" is used, we are taking our cues from Scripture and *Merriam-Webster's Collegiate Dictionary (10th Edition)*. Know that a mystery is a religious truth that one can truly know only by revelation and may not be fully understood. A mystic relates to the mysterious, has a feeling of awe or wonder, and is a follower of the mystical way of life. A mystical way of life is having a spiritual meaning of reality. It involves having direct communion with God our ultimate reality.

Mysticism is the belief that direct knowledge of God, spiritual truth, or ultimate reality can be attained through experience. According to Dr. Elizabeth Alvilda Petroff, mysticism has been called "the science of the love of God," and "the life which aims at union with God." Its emphasis is on the spiritual life as a progressive climb—sometimes a steep and arduous one.

Always remember that the Messiah's followers make manifest the mystery of Christ in you, the hope of glory, in word and deed. The antidote to the "Mystery of Iniquity" (1 Thessalonians 2:7), "Mystery Babylon" (Revelation 17:5), and the "mystery of the woman and the beast" (Revelation 17:7) are literally found in the mysteries of God the Father and of Christ, so let's redeem "the mystic". The Righteous Order of Melchizedek restores all things that can be redeemed. Having direct communion with God and His ultimate reality through experience is not only redeemable, but it's also divine and sublime. Next time you hear the word "mystic" think of knowing the love of God, and displaying this unlimited, exquisite mystery for all to see.

Thoughts

The Way Of Wisdom

1. Look up Scriptures regarding various words and phrases that accompany the untranslated ALEF-TAV (את) in Micah 5:1. For instance:

"Judge of Israel" (Mic. 5:1). Hint: Psalms 9:8 and Psalms 50:6-7.

_____

_____

_____

_____

"Cheek" (Mic. 5:1). Hint: Job 16:10.

_____

_____

_____

_____

2. Look up Scriptures regarding various words and phrases that accompany the untranslated ALEF-TAV (את) in Zechariah 12:10. For instance:

"Spirit of Grace" (Zech. 12:10). Hint: Hebrews 10:29.

_____

_____

_____

_____

"Pierced" (Zech. 12:10). Hint: Isaiah 53:5.

_____

_____

_____

_____

_____

3. Research the implications of the prophetic declaration made in Micah 5:1— *"They will strike [ALEF-TAV (את)] the judge of Israel with a rod on the cheek."* Ask yourself questions like what does striking a person on the cheek mean? What happens when someone strikes a judge or ruler?

_____

_____

_____

_____

_____

4. Look up Scriptures that contain the term "mystery." Read them in context and contemplate what they mean at a surface level and beyond. Note: This list is not all-inclusive. If you feel led, find the other Bible verses that include the word "mystery."

God's disciples know the **mystery** of the kingdom of God (Mark 4:11):

_____

_____

_____

_____

_____

Don't be ignorant of the **mystery** happening to Israel (Rom. 11:25):

_____

_____

_____

_____

_____

Revelation of the **mystery** kept secret since the world began (Rom. 16:25):

_____

_____

_____

_____

We speak the wisdom of God in a **mystery**, which God ordained before the ages for our glory (2 Cor. 2:7):

_____

_____

_____

_____

The **mystery** of God's will according to His good pleasure (Eph. 1:9):

_____

_____

_____

_____

The fellowship of the **mystery** hidden in God (Eph. 3:9):

_____

_____

_____

_____

The great **mystery** of Christ and the church (Eph. 5:32):

_____

_____

_____

_____

The **mystery** of the gospel (Eph. 6:19):

_____

_____

_____

_____

The **mystery** of lawlessness is already at work (2 Thess. 2:7):

_____

_____

_____

_____

Holding the **mystery** of faith with a pure conscience (1 Tim. 3:9):

_____

_____

_____

_____

Great is the **mystery** of godliness (1 Tim. 3:16):

_____

_____

_____

_____

Mystery, Babylon the Great (Rev. 17:5):

_____

_____

_____

_____

5. Look up Scriptures that contain the term "mysteries." Read them in context and contemplate what they mean at a surface level and beyond. Hint: Matthew 13:11; Luke 8:10; 1 Corinthians 4:1; 1 Corinthians 13:2; 1 Corinthians 14:2.

_____

_____

_____

_____

ALEF

WISDOM THREE

א ALEF

ALEF/ALEPH (א)

ALEF (א) is the first *Hebrew Living™ Letter* of the Alef-Bet. It's pronounced *ah-lef*. It can also be spelled ALEPH. In simplest terms, ALEF has a numerical value of 1 and its sound is silent. Since ALEF(א) is a silent letter, it points to the mysteries of the oneness of God. Every aspect of the form of the Hebrew letter ALEF/ALEPH (א) has been divinely designed by God Himself to teach us heavenly truths. ALEF (א) signifies the Most High God and His glory. Hebrew is a language read from right to left. If a person lists the Hebrew Alphabet in ascending order, all the other Hebrew letters face away from the first letter ALEF. It is like they are not to gaze at His divine glory, which corresponds to *Exodus 33:23—You may see My back, but My face may not be seen.*"[2]

The ancient pictograph for ALEF (א) agrees with the meaning of its name. In ancient Hebrew ALEF means an ox or a bull, which symbolizes strength, a leader, a father, or what is first. [3]

ALEF (א) IN ALEF-TAV (את)

Messiah Yeshua is the exquisite ALEF (א) IN ALEF-TAV (את).

> " *[4] Grace to you and peace from Him who is and who was and who is to come, and from the seven Spirits who are before His throne, [5] and from Jesus Christ, the faithful witness, the firstborn from the dead, and the ruler over the kings of the earth. To Him who loved us and washed us from our sins in His own blood, [6] and has made us kings and priests to His God and Father, to Him be glory and dominion forever and ever. Amen. [7] Behold, He is coming with clouds, and every eye will see Him, even they who pierced Him. And all the tribes of the earth will mourn because of Him. Even so, Amen. [8] 'I am the Alpha [ALEF] and the Omega [TAV], the Beginning and the End,' says the Lord, 'who is and who was and who is to come, the Almighty'" (Revelation 1:4-8 Additions mine).*

Since ALEF (א) in ancient Hebrew is a picture of an ox, some say that the name of the letter ALEF (א) comes from the Hebrew word *alluph*, which means an ox or bullock. "John MacMillian states in *Christ in the Hebrew Alphabet*, 'Aleph is the animal ready for service and ready for sacrifice.' "[4]

---

[2] *Understanding the Alef-Beis: Insights into the Hebrew Letters and Methods for Interpreting Them* by Dovid Leitner, p. 187
[3] *Hebrew Word Pictures* by Frank T. Seekins, Alef, p. 12
[5] *Messiah and His Hebrew Alphabet* by Dick Mills & David Michael, p. 2

"The Servant" is a Messianic title, which is connected to the Lamb of God being led to slaughter (i.e., the Cross), and Him not opening His mouth (Isa. 53:7; Acts 8:32):

> *"Behold! My Servant whom I uphold, My Elect One in whom My soul delights! I have put My Spirit upon Him; He will bring forth justice to the Gentiles. ² He will not cry out, nor raise His voice . . ." (Isaiah 42:1-2a).*

The Hebraic understanding of "the Servant" remembers the Servant as the heavenly high priest. Therefore, the servants of the Lord were high priests of the Most High God who entered the Holy of Holies to learn the secrets of the various kingdoms of God.

Yeshua Ha Mashiach (Jesus Christ) is the Mature Head of the Body of Christ (Eph. 4:15). He is also the High Priest of the Righteous Order of Melchizedek (Heb. 2:17; 4:14-15; 5:1,5,10; 6:20; 7:26; 8:1; 9:11; 10:21). What's the role of the Mature Body of Christ connected to the Mature Head as the High Priest, if they are in fact one (John 17:23)? Being one necessitates that the members of the Mature Body of Christ are high priests too. This is hinted at in Revelation 1:5-6 and Revelation 5:9-10, which tells us that Yeshua has made us kings and priests. However, these precious souls are only high priests made after the Order of Melchizedek through their oneness connection to ALEF-TAV (את). They cannot be kings and priests of His eternal order otherwise.

This does not diminish, nor replace the fact, that Yeshua is the Highest Priest made after the Order of Melchizedek. When Yeshua's flesh was crucified, the veil was torn in God's Temple and a new and living way was made for you and me to access the Presence of the Most High God. This access to the Holy of Holiest beyond the veil is a privilege of a High Priest—a High Priest of the House of God. Yeshua is the High Priest of the Order of Melchizedek over the House of God. Hebrews 10 puts it this way:

> *"Having therefore, brethren, boldness to enter into the holiest by the blood of Jesus, By a new and living way, which He has consecrated for us, through the veil, that is to say, His flesh; And having a High Priest over the house of God; Let us draw near with a true heart in full assurance of faith, having our hearts sprinkled from an evil conscience, and our bodies washed with pure water. Let us hold fast the profession of our faith without wavering; (for he is faithful that promised;) And let us consider one another to provoke unto love and to good works" (Hebrews 10:19-24).*

First John 2:6 says it this way. We will walk in the same manner as Yeshua did. This includes walking as a High Priest of the Order of Melchizedek. We are the Priesthood of All Believers that is made up of High Priests in an Eternal Priesthood. This Holy Eternal Priesthood is not based on a person's ancestry but *"on the basis of the power of an indestructible life. For it is declared: 'You are a priest forever, in the Order of Melchizedek'"* (Hebrews 7:16-17).

In this Kingdom Day, God's mature/maturing sons will follow in the Order of Melchizedek High Priest's (Messiah Yeshua's) footsteps, because we are one with the Servant who knows how to maintain the Almighty's Eternal Covenant of Peace. Yeshua did not come to the world to be served, but to serve and to sacrificially give His life for the reconciliation and redemption of the world:

" 25 But Jesus called them to Himself and said, 'You know that the rulers of the Gentiles lord it over them, and those who are great exercise authority over them. 26 Yet it shall not be so among you; but whoever desires to become great among you, let him be your servant. 27 And whoever desires to be first among you, let him be your slave— 28 just as the Son of Man did not come to be served, but to serve, and to give His life a ransom for many' " (Matthew 20:25-28).

The first thing that usually comes to mind with an ox is the catchphrase "strong as an ox." Throughout human history, teams of oxen or a single ox have been used to plow fields and pull heavy loads. As a burden bearer, Messiah Yeshua instructs His people:

" 28 Come to Me, all you who labor and are heavy laden, and I will give you rest. 29 Take My yoke upon you and learn from Me, for I am gentle and lowly in heart, and you will find rest for your souls. 30 For My yoke is easy and My burden is light" (Matthew 11:28-30).

It is the commandments about priests, sacrifices, and altars that gives us hope and confidence that the sacrifice of Yeshua of Nazareth has a binding effect and is able to cover our sins before the Living God. To undermine the truth of God's Word about priests, altars, and sacrifices is to undercut the once-for-all sacrifice of Yeshua (Jesus), as the Lamb of God who takes away the sins of the world.

" 11 But Christ came as High Priest of the good things to come, with the greater and more perfect tabernacle not made with hands, that is, not of this creation. 12 Not with the blood of goats and calves, but <u>with His own blood He entered the Most Holy Place once for all, having obtained eternal redemption</u>. 13 For if the blood of bulls and goats and the ashes of a heifer, sprinkling the unclean, sanctifies for the purifying of the flesh, 14 how much more shall the blood of Christ, who through the eternal Spirit offered Himself without spot to God, cleanse your conscience from dead works to serve the living God? 15 And for this reason He is the Mediator of the new covenant, by means of death, for the redemption of the transgressions under the first covenant, that those who are called may receive the promise of the eternal inheritance" (Hebrews 9:11-15).

There are thirteen sacrifices according to the teaching of the Messiah,[5] which He fulfills, as the High Priest of the Order of Melchizedek (Heb. 5:5-6):

1) **olah** (עֹלָה) • The *olah* is the whole burnt offering, which is a voluntary offering given exclusively to the Lord. It is also called the elevation offering or ascension offering. No part of it is used by any earthly priest or anyone else. Notice that the Hebrew word *olah* (עֹלָה) is made up of three Hebrew letters whose incredible word picture tells us that the Shepherd brings forth. If you are going to make a burnt offering from the herd (a bull) or the flock (a lamb), you would go to the shepherd to request: Select one for me. The Shepherd would then make a judgment as to what is the best one for you and he would bring it to you. Who is the Great Shepherd? Yeshua (Heb. 13:20). Has He not brought us the perfect sacrifice of Himself for our sins? Remember the sacrificial oxen or sheep had to be perfect—without blemish. Yeshua is the living embodiment of the *olah* offering.

---

[5]*Leviticus.* Third Edition Teaching Series by Monte Judah. CD 1 of 11. Lev. 1:1-6:7. *Lion and Lamb Ministries.*

2) **minchah** (מנחה) • The *minchah* is a meal offering made from either flour, bread, or cakes. It is sometimes called the grain offering. Doesn't the Messiah say that He is the true bread of heaven? (John 6:32).

3) **ḥatat** (חַטָּאת) • The *ḥatat* is a sin offering only made for unintentional sins. It has nothing to do with a sin that is intentional. It is a sin of omission or a mistake. Messiah Yeshua is our sin offering for unintentional and intentional sins (Heb. 10:5-9).

4) **nesekh** (נֶסֶךְ) • The *nesekh* is a drink offering which is usually wine. It's an offering of joy. Every time we take communion in remembrance of Him, we speak to the presence of the Messiah being our real joy. His redemptive blood shed for us is the cup that accompanies the bread. It also represents His Blood—His family (1 Cor. 11:23-26).

5) **tenufah** (תנופה) • The *tenufah* is the wave offering, which can be sheaves of grain, branches, or loaves that are waved before the Lord. It is a more refined version of the grain offering. Just like a wave offering, we lift up our hands to the Messiah in worship, which is the offering that's raised up. The Messiah referred to the wave offering as our evening sacrifice (Psa. 141:2).

6) **asham** (אשם) • The *asham* is the guilt offering, which is an offering made by leaders who have unintentionally made a mistake. Messiah Yeshua is our guilt offering because we recognize that He is the leader or the Head of the Body of Christ. Those who recognize His leadership have to align with the Heavenly Father's perfect will, like Yeshua did (John 5:19). When we do this by doing our best as well as trusting Him completely, all the requirements of a guilt offering for a leader who makes a mistake are fulfilled by endeavoring to follow His leadership to the best of one's ability.

7) **millu** (מִלֻּא) • The *millu* is the ordination offering that represents dedication. The name "Messiah" means the promised "anointed one" or Christ, the Savior. [6] Anointing oil is poured out at an ordination. By Yeshua being called the Anointed One, you call the Messiah the ordination offering.

8) **shelamim** (שְׁלָמִים) • The *shelamim* is the peace offering, which usually involves other parties. It's an agreement between you and others that's acknowledged before the Lord. The Messiah Himself is our peace (Eph. 2:14-15). Yeshua is the best peace offering for you. He imparts the peace that surpasses all understanding (Phil. 4:6-7).

9) **todah** (תּוֹדָה) • The *todah* is the thanksgiving offering, which is generally given at the completion of some major task or effort. The thanksgiving offering really means a praise or thanksgiving. Messiah Yeshua is the subject of praise and thanksgiving. Paul tells us to continually offer the sacrifice of praise to God by way of Messiah Yeshua, and to give thanks in Christ, as the fruit of our lips (Heb. 13:15).

---

[6] "Messiah." dictionary.com

Thoughts

10) *nedabah* (נְדָבָה) • The *nedabah* is the freewill offering, which involves the Lord in a great celebration. The freewill offering is really about love. Everyone loves a celebration! If you understand the reason for the celebration, your expression of love and joy is magnified. Messiah Yeshua is the love offering that causes us to be full of joy: *"Looking unto Jesus, the author and finisher of our faith, who for the joy that was set before Him endured the cross, despising the shame, and has sat down at the right hand of the throne of God"* (Heb. 12:2).

11) *neder* (נֶדֶר) • The *neder* is the votive offering, which is connected to a vow. You made a vow and completed it; therefore, you offer a votive offering. The Lord Jesus Christ has vowed to save you. He has proclaimed, I will deliver you. I will never leave, nor forsake you (Heb. 13:5). Never! Wow! Now that's a vow! Messiah Yeshua is the highest form of a vow offering that we have.

12) *terumah* (תְּרוּמָה) • The *terumah* is the heave offering, which is a true contribution from the heart primarily. The Messiah expressly taught us that the *terumah* offering that Moses gave was a willing heart. The congregation of the Living God is formed by having a willing heart, which is being wholehearted in all you are and all you do (Mark 12:33; Eph. 3:17-19).

13) *azkarah* (אַזְכָּרָה) • The *azkarah* is the memorial offering, which is made in remembrance of something. Messiah Yeshua is our memorial offering. Every time we take the bread and wine of common union—communion—we are remembering the sacrificial work of the Messiah on the Cross (1 Cor. 11:26).

Before the New Covenant, the Jews did not get saved by offering sacrifices. No scripture teaches this. What was taught is that there is no sacrifice for intentional sin that can be brought by man. Before the Law was given, Scripture teaches us that if God brings a lamb for you, it will cover all your intentional and unintentional sins, so you can pass from death to life. It is the Lamb of God sacrifice portrayed when Abraham and Isaac went up Mount Moriah to worship God (Gen. 22).

When Yeshua came to do His sacrifice as the Lamb of God sacrifice (John 1:29) once(ALEF)-for-all, He did not change any of the other offerings. He did not make them go away. They are still true. They are still with us today because Yeshua Himself fulfills them:

> ***"Do not think that I came to destroy the Law or the Prophets. I did not come to destroy but to fulfill" (Matthew 5:17).***

Thoughts

The Way Of Wisdom

1. Research and contemplate various significant points that supplements Revelation 1:8's declaration "*I am the Alpha* [ALEF] *and the Omega* [TAV]." For example:

"*Who is and who was and who is to come, the Almighty*" (Rev.1:8):

_____

_____

_____

"*Jesus Christ, the faithful witness*" (Rev.1:5): . . . *the firstborn from the dead, and the ruler over the kings of the earth. To Him who loved us and washed us from our sins in His own blood*" (Rev.1:5):

_____

_____

_____

"*Jesus Christ . . . has made us kings and priests to His God and Father*" (Rev.1:6):

_____

_____

_____

2. How can people be high priests made after the Order of Melchizedek? Hint: Oneness.

_____

_____

_____

3. Why is the Order of Melchizedek an eternal order? Study the context of Hebrews 7:16.

_____

_____

_____

4. What are various aspects of kings and priests? For example, kings rule. Priests mediate.

_____

_____

_____

5. Messiah Yeshua came as a Servant to serve, not to be served. What truths can we glean from researching the term "servant" in Scripture? Take for instance:

King David repeatedly calls himself "servant" in the Book of Psalms while Messiah Yeshua builds His Kingdom upon the Throne of David (Isa. 9:7):

_____

_____

_____

Abraham, Isaac, Jacob, and Moses were God's servants (Exo. 4:10; 32:13; Mal. 4:4; Heb. 3:5):

_____

_____

_____

Servants of Christ are stewards of the mysteries of God (1 Cor. 4:1.):

_____

_____

_____

6. What burdens can you personally cast on our Burden Bearer, Messiah Yeshua (Matt. 11:28-30) and how can you cast your cares upon Him (1 Pet. 5:6-7)?

_____

_____

_____

7. Why do you think that the *olah* (עֹלָה) offering is also called the elevation offering or ascension offering?

_____

_____

_____

ALEF (א)

Meditate upon the ALEF-TAV (את) treasures of wisdom that you have learned about ALEF (א), which represents burden bearing, service, and sacrifice. What is most meaningful to you and why?

PRACTICE WRITING ALEF

● Pronounced *ah-lef* ●

Draw the diagonal line VAV (ו) first. Then draw the upper YUD (י) and lower YUD (י).

is the letter of fire—AYSH/ESH
(אֵשׁ)—which is the substance that
consumes the sacrifice. Fundamentally,
fire represents the Presence of God, as
revealed to Moses in the burning bush
and in the Pillar of Fire protecting His
people in the wilderness. Behold, אֵשׁ
is the light, heat, energy, and power of
transformation of a burning heart who
loves the LORD God with all their
heart, soul, and strength.

BET

WISDOM FOUR

ב

BET

BET/BEIS/BAIT (ב)

BET (ב) is the second *Hebrew Living™ Letter* of the Alef-Bet that can be pronounced as *bet* or *bayt*. It can also be pronounced *bais*. BET (ב) has a numerical value of 2. In actuality, BET has a "b" sound as in "boy" when there is a dagesh (dot) in the middle of the letter and a "v" sound as in "vet" without a dagesh. For simplicity's sake, we will only focus on the "b."

The pictograph for BET (ב) is a tent, dwelling place, or house. Let's first contemplate a few Scriptures for each, which paints a picture of our temporary earthly house, as a tent, that points to a more permanent eternal house, which is a dwelling place of God in the Spirit.

TENT:

"The voice of rejoicing and salvation is in the <u>tents</u> of the righteous; The right hand of the Lord does valiantly" (Psalms 118:14).

"The house of the wicked will be overthrown, But the <u>tent</u> of the upright will flourish" (Proverbs 14:11).

"For we know that if our earthly house, this <u>tent</u>, is destroyed, we have a building from God, a house not made with hands, eternal in the heavens. ²For in this we groan, earnestly desiring to be clothed with our habitation which is from heaven, ³if indeed, having been clothed, we shall not be found naked. ⁴For we who are in this <u>tent</u> groan, being burdened, not because we want to be unclothed, but further clothed, that mortality may be swallowed up by life. ⁵Now He who has prepared us for this very thing is God, who also has given us the Spirit as a guarantee" (2 Corinthians 5:1-5).

DWELLING PLACE:

"⁹Because you have made the Lord, who is my refuge, Even the Most High, your <u>dwelling place</u>, ¹⁰No evil shall befall you, Nor shall any plague come near your <u>dwelling</u>; ¹¹For He shall give His angels charge over you, To keep you in all your ways" (Psalms 91:9-11).

"For the Lord has chosen Zion; He has desired it for His <u>dwelling place</u>: ¹⁴"This is My resting place forever; Here I will dwell, for I have desired it" (Psalms 132:13-14).

"Jesus Christ Himself being the chief cornerstone, ²¹ in whom the whole building, being fitted together, grows into a holy temple in the Lord, ²² in whom you also are being built together for a <u>dwelling place</u> of God in the Spirit" (Ephesians 2:20b-21).

HOUSE:

"⁶ Pray for the peace of Jerusalem: 'May they prosper who love you. ⁷ Peace be within your walls, Prosperity within your palaces.' ⁸ For the sake of my brethren and companions, I will now say, 'Peace be within you.' ⁹ Because of the <u>house</u> of the Lord our God I will seek your good" (Psalms 122:6-9).

"The wicked are overthrown and are no more, But the <u>house</u> of the righteous will stand" (Proverbs 12:7).

"Therefore, holy brethren, partakers of the heavenly calling, consider the Apostle and High Priest of our confession, Christ Jesus, ² who was faithful to Him who appointed Him, as Moses also was faithful in all His <u>house</u>. ³ For this One has been counted worthy of more glory than Moses, inasmuch as He who built the <u>house</u> has more honor than the <u>house</u>. ⁴ For every <u>house</u> is built by someone, but He who built all things is God. ⁵ And Moses indeed was faithful in all His <u>house</u> as a servant, for a testimony of those things which would be spoken afterward, ⁶ but Christ as a Son over His own <u>house</u>, whose <u>house</u> we are if we hold fast the confidence and the rejoicing of the hope firm to the end" (Hebrews 3:1-6).

When BET (בּ) is a prefix for a word, it carries the meaning of "in" and suggests that God has the intention of abiding within the realm of His creation: *"For behold, the Kingdom of God is <u>in</u> your midst [within you]"* (Luke 17:21 $_{NASB\,[KJV]}$). *"I <u>in</u> them, and You <u>in</u> Me; that they may be made perfect <u>in</u> one, and that the world may know that You have sent Me, and loved them as You have loved Me"* (John 17:23). Being prefixed with BET can also carry the meaning of a person being "in Christ."

IN CHRIST:

"¹ There is therefore now no condemnation to those who are <u>in Christ</u> Jesus, who do not walk according to the flesh, but according to the Spirit. ² For the law of the Spirit of life <u>in Christ</u> Jesus has made me free from the law of sin and death" (Romans 8:1-2).

"²⁶ The mystery which has been hidden from ages and from generations, but now has been revealed to His saints. ²⁷ To them God willed to make known what are the riches of the glory of this mystery among the Gentiles: which is Christ in you, the hope of glory. ²⁸ Him we preach, warning every man and teaching every man in all wisdom, that we may present every man perfect <u>in Christ</u> Jesus" (Colossians 1:26-28).

Scripture begins with the Book of Genesis. The Book of Genesis is named after its first word in Hebrew *"bereshit"* בְּרֵאשִׁית, which is commonly translated "in a beginning." This speaks of the whole of creation as a house—a BET—in relation to God. The word *bereshit* is always written large at the beginning of a Torah scroll. The Hebrews say that this is to teach humanity that they should always seek the first ALEF (א) first—

The Creator. With BET (בּ) signifying Creation and the Creator, we note that the root of the first word in the Bible *Bereshit*—בְּרֵאשִׁית—is *rosh*, which means head. The prefix is a *bet* while the last two letters of the word *Bereshit* are YUD (י) and TAV (ת), which together spell *bayis*—the Hebrew word for house. In the beginning, when God created the world, his *taavah*, תַּאֲוָה (desire), was that the head (which is God) should dwell in the *bayis*, His home. And how does one make a home for God? By living the letter BET (בּ). BET (בֵּית) is all about the House of God. A place where everyone is at home. To live the letter BET (בּ), we need to resonate at the frequency of the Word of God.

BET (בּ) IN ALEF-TAV (את)

You and I can personally choose to engage the essence of Messiah Yeshua—the Word of God—contained within the Hebrew letter BET (בּ).

ALEF (א) teaches us about the Oneness of God. From BET (בּ), we learn about the House that God built with His Hebrew letter building blocks. ALEF-TAV (את) houses Creation, or we could say ALEF-TAV (את) is the House of Creation—where all things have been created through Him, for Him, and in Him. The first chapter of Colossians puts it this way:

*"15 He is the image of the invisible God, the firstborn of all creation: 16 for by Him all things were created, both in the heavens and on earth, visible and invisible, whether thrones, or dominions, or rulers, or authorities—all things have been created through Him and for Him. 17 He is before all things, and in Him all things hold together. 18 He is also the head of the body, the church; and He is the beginning, the firstborn from the dead, so that He Himself will come to have first place in everything. 19 For it was the Father's good pleasure for all the fullness to dwell in Him, 20 and through Him to reconcile all things to Himself, whether things on earth or things in heaven, having made peace through the blood of His cross" (Colossians 1:15-20*_{NASB}*).*

Several names and titles of God begin with BET, but it is primarily used for the Son of God (בן אלהים—*ben-Elohim*). The Aramaic word for son is *"bar"* while the word for create is *"bara."* If we separate the letters within the word *"bara,"* we have *"bar"* (son) and *"a"*- ALEF (father). This points us to the Only Begotten Son of our Heavenly Father (ALEF) and to John Chapter 1:

*"In the beginning was the Word, and the Word was with God, and the Word was God and the Word was made flesh and dwelt among us (and we beheld His glory, the glory as of the only begotten of the Father), full of grace and truth" (John 1:1,14*_{KJV}*).*

It is significant that when we combine the Hebrew word for father *(av)* with the word for son *(ben)*, we get the Hebrew word for stone (אבן—*even)*. Just like the molecules in a stone are so intertwined that they appear to be one, so are the Heavenly Father and His Son. Yeshua's oneness with His Father is pictured metaphorically as the Stone of Israel, which the builders rejected that has become the chief cornerstone (Matt. 21:42).

The unfathomable mystery of heaven and earth being united in the same body is portrayed in Yeshua when He walked this earth as the Son of God. When Yeshua was conceived, the Heavenly Father's nature was fused with that of the woman. Blood can only be transmitted through the seed of a man to the egg of a woman. In Yeshua's case, the Father put His life in the form of blood into the womb of Mary. He used the instrument of His blood to unite human and divine nature. Eternity penetrated time and inhabited a body for the first time at Messiah Yeshua's conception.

This is eternal life. Not only are we talking about a life that does not die, but the very nature of God penetrates our humanity and unites us with Him. The Son of God became flesh and dwelt among us (John 1:14). He continues to become flesh through His Body, specifically those in the Righteous Order of Melchizedek that are made like unto the Son of God (Heb. 7:3). The Seventh Day Transfiguration of Man is the One New Man in Christ (i.e., the Messiah) made up of mature and maturing sons.

The journey of those who are manifesting being part of the royal priesthood of ONE LOVE will literally increase the ten-percent deposit of the Holy Spirit within them in amount, magnitude, and degree to the fullness of the stature of Christ by living a crucified life unto the knowledge of the Son of God via the Seven Spirits of God. There is a Kingdom time and Kingdom place where *"we all will come in the unity of the faith, and of the knowledge of the Son of God, unto a perfect man, unto the measure of the stature of the fullness of Christ"* (Ephesians 4:13 $_{KJV}$). Notice how it says, *"we all come . . . unto the measure of the stature of the fullness of Christ,"* because this is both an individual and corporate work of His Spirit by the Blood according to the Father's heart.

We know that he who believes that Yeshua is the Son of God, and in His death, burial, and resurrection overcomes the world: *"For whatever is born of God overcomes the world. And this is the victory that has overcome the world—our faith. Who is he who overcomes the world, but he who believes that Jesus is the Son of God?"* *(1 John 5:4-5)*. We also know that the Melchizedek Company is made like unto the Son of God, so pay attention when you study Scripture to the phrase "Son of God," because His Royal Priestly Order of Melchizedek will walk in the same manner as the Son of God manifesting the excellencies of His Everlasting Kingdom.

The kings and priests made after the Order of Melchizedek are leading their own inner fire bride forth so that they can attain oneness with their Beloved High Priest Messiah Yeshua (Heb. 6:20). When His royal priesthood realizes their bridal oneness, it is an *echad* oneness (plurality in one) where no one loses their individuality. They complete one another. It is in this place, they dwell in unity and become the Lord's tent mate.

Revelation 21:9 speaks of the Lamb of God's wife, His Bride. The Greek word for "dwell" in Revelation 21:3 is *skay-no'-o* (σκηνόω). It is defined as fixing one's tabernacle, abiding in a tabernacle, living in a tent, encamping, residing, or dwelling. *Skay-no'-o* is specific to Revelation 21:3, it means to be one's tent-mate.

> *"Then I saw a new heaven and a new earth; for the first heaven and the first earth passed away, and there is no longer any sea. And I saw the holy city, New Jerusalem, coming down out of heaven from God, prepared as a bride adorned for her husband. And I heard a loud voice from the throne, saying, 'Behold, the tabernacle of God is among the people, and He will <u>dwell</u> among them, and they shall be His people, and God Himself will be among them'"* (Revelation 21:1-3 $_{NASB}$).

The Way Of Wisdom

1. What are some of the ways that you can live the letter BET (בּ), i.e., resonate at the frequency of ALEF-TAV (את) who is the Word of God?

_____

_____

_____

2. What makes ALEF-TAV (את) both the House of Creation and the Creator Himself? Hint: Colossians 1:15-20; Ephesians 4:15-16; Hebrews 1:1-3.

_____

_____

_____

3. How can you be made like unto the Son of God? Hint: Look up the phrase "Son of God" in Scripture, seek to understand it in context; and then, and apply it to your own life.

Live by faith of the **Son of God** (Gal. 2:20):

_____

_____

_____

Attain the knowledge of the **Son of God** (Eph. 4:13):

_____

_____

_____

The **Son of God** destroys the works of the devil (1 John 3:8):

_____

_____

_____

Those who confess that Jesus is the **Son of God**, God remains in Him and he in God (1 John 4:15):

_____

_____

_____

Those who believe Jesus is the **Son of God** overcome the world (1 John 5:5):

_____

_____

_____

Those who have the **Son of God** have life, and those who believe in His Name have eternal life (1 John 5:12-13):

_____

_____

_____

The **Son of God** has eyes like a flame of fire (Rev. 2:18):

_____

_____

_____

4. Recall the combination of the Hebrew word for father *(av)* with the word for son *(ben)* results in the Hebrew word for stone (אבן - *even)*. What are some Scriptures that carry the Father/Son oneness concept via the words "stone" or rock"?

Stone of Israel (Gen. 49:24):

_____

_____

_____

There is no rock like our God (1 Sam. 2:2):

_____

_____

_____

Moses struck the rock at Horeb as instructed by God. Water came out of the rock in the Wilderness so the people could drink (Exo. 17:6):

_____

_____

_____

There is a place by God on the rock. Moses is put in the cleft of the rock as His glory passes by (Exo. 33:21-22):

_____

_____

_____

The Rock's work is perfect and His ways faithful, righteous, and just (Deut. 32:1-4):

_____

_____

_____

The Lord is my rock, my fortress, my shield, my stronghold, and my savior in whom I take refuge (Psa. 18:2):

_____

_____

_____

The spiritual rock that followed the Israelites in the Wilderness was Christ. Note: Hebrew history records this event. (1 Cor. 10:4):

_____

_____

_____

5. ALEF-TAV (את) and His Bride (the New Jerusalem) are shown to tabernacle together in Revelation 21:3. What does it mean to you to be one's tent mate—_skay-no'-o (σκηνόω)_?

_____

_____

_____

6. What is the importance that the root of the first word in the Bible _Bereshit_—בְּרֵאשִׁית—is _rosh_, which means head?

_____

_____

_____

BET (בּ)

What ALEF-TAV (את) nugget of wisdom about the BET (בּ) impacts you the most?

PRACTICE WRITING BET

◆ Pronounced *bet* or *bay-t* ◆

Start at the top to draw across and then down to the baseline.

Second, draw the bottom horizontal line. Then add the dagesh dot at the end.

בּ בּ בּ בּ בּ בּ בּ

is a house firmly set on earth. The dot in the middle of בּ is called a dagesh, which represents one who lives within. Jacob was the man whose head rested upon the Rock where he had a vivid dream of a ladder reaching up from earth to heaven with angels ascending and descending on it. God proclaimed to Jacob, *"Behold, I am with you and will keep you wherever you go" (Gen. 28:15)*. The ladder to the gate of heaven was Jacob's own DNA, having been made in God's own image. Behold, God is with you, and you are the House of God.

WISDOM FIVE

ג

GIMEL

GIMEL/GIMMEL (ג)

GIMEL (ג) is the third *Hebrew Living™ Letter* of the Alef-Bet. It's pronounced *geeh-mel* with a "g" sound as in "girl." GIMEL (ג) has the numerical value of 3, which means that the Hebrews use it for the number 3.

The ancient pictograph for GIMEL (ג) agrees with the meaning of its name. In ancient Hebrew GIMEL means a camel, which symbolizes a camel or beast, provision, lifted up (like a camel rising from its knees), or self-will or pride (like an obstinate camel).[7]

GIMEL (ג) IN ALEF-TAV (את)

You and I can personally choose to engage the essence of Messiah Yeshua—the Word of God—contained within the Hebrew letter GIMEL (ג). First, let us focus on the provision part of ALEF-TAV (את). The faith of Abraham says God Himself will provide a lamb for the burnt offering on Mount Moriah:

> " *⁴ On the third day Abraham raised his eyes and saw the place from a distance. ⁵ Then Abraham said to his young men, 'Stay here with the donkey, and I and the boy will go over there; and we will worship and return to you.' ⁶ And Abraham took the wood for the burnt offering and laid it on his son Isaac, and he took in his hand the fire and the knife. So the two of them walked on together. ⁷ Isaac spoke to his father Abraham and said, 'My father!' And he said, 'Here I am, my son.' And he said, 'Look, the fire and the wood, but where is the lamb for the burnt offering?' ⁸ Abraham said, 'God will provide for Himself the lamb for the burnt offering, my son.' So the two of them walked on together"* (Genesis 22:4-8 ₙₐₛB).

At the time, Abraham was 137 years old and Isaac was 36 so they both ascended Mount Moriah voluntarily to offer up an elevation offering solely to God. This was a foreshadowing of Yeshua carrying the wood of the cross for the burnt offering of Himself while His Heavenly Father took the knife (an instrument for slaughter) and fire. Yeshua's forerunner—John the Baptist—revealed three baptisms: water, Holy Spirit, and fire. *"As for me, I baptize you with water for repentance, but He who is coming after me is mightier than I, and I am not fit to remove His sandals; He will baptize you with the Holy Spirit and fire"* (Matthew 3:11 ₙₐₛB). The Cross was ALEF-TAV's baptism of fire.

---

[7] *Hebrew Word Pictures* by Frank T. Seekins, Gimel, p. 20

"The (גימל), *gimmel*, is cognate [same original root] to (גמל), *gamol*, which means to nourish until completely ripe, as in (וַיִּגְמֹל שְׁקֵדִים), it produced mature almonds (Numbers 17:23)." [8] The greatness of GIMEL (ג) is ALEF-TAV (את)—the Son of God—being the lifeline (nourishment) for the Body of Christ:

> *"Till we all come to the unity of the faith and of the knowledge of the Son of God, to a perfect man, to the measure of the stature of the fullness of Christ;* [14] *that we should no longer be children, tossed to and fro and carried about with every wind of doctrine, by the trickery of men, in the cunning craftiness of deceitful plotting,* [15] *but, speaking the truth in love, <u>may grow up in all things into Him who is the head</u>—Christ—* [16] *from whom the whole body, joined and knit together by what every joint supplies, according to the effective working by which every part does its share, causes growth of the body for the edifying of itself in love" (Ephesians 4:13-16).*

> *"Let no one cheat you of your reward, taking delight in false humility and worship of angels, intruding into those things which he has not seen, vainly puffed up by his fleshly mind,* [19] *and not holding fast to <u>the Head, from whom all the body, nourished</u> and knit together by joints and ligaments, grows with the increase that is from God" (Colossians 2:18-19).*

> *"I am the true vine, and My Father is the vinedresser.* [2] *Every branch in Me that does not bear fruit He takes away; and every branch that bears fruit He prunes, that it may bear more fruit. . . .* [4] *Abide in Me, and I in you. As the branch cannot bear fruit of itself, unless it abides in the vine, neither can you, unless you abide in Me.* [5] *I am the vine, you are the branches. <u>He who abides in Me, and I in him, bears much fruit</u>; for without Me you can do nothing" (John 15:1-5).*

GIMEL (ג) is the first letter in the ascending alphabet sequence that is adorned with three crowns. BET (ב) in the ALEF-TAV (את) connects us to the Son of God—Messiah Yeshua. GIMEL (ג) connects us to the perfect provision of His Kingdom.

> *"* [31] *Do not worry then, saying, 'What are we to eat?' or 'What are we to drink?' or 'What are we to wear for clothing?'* [32] *For the Gentiles eagerly seek all these things; for your heavenly Father knows that you need all these things.* [33] *But <u>seek first His kingdom and His righteousness, and all these things will be provided to you</u>" (Matthew 6:31-33 NASB).*

> *"Whoever believes that Jesus is the Christ is born of God, and everyone who loves Him who begot also loves Him who is begotten of Him.* [2] *By this we know that we love the children of God, when we love God and keep His commandments.* [3] *For this is the love of God, that we keep His commandments. And His commandments are not burdensome.* [4] *For whatever is born of God overcomes the world. And this is the victory that has overcome the world—our faith.* [5] *Who is he who overcomes the world, but he who believes that Jesus is the Son of God?* [6] *This is He who came by water and blood—Jesus Christ; not only by water, but by water and blood. And it is the Spirit who bears witness, because the Spirit is truth.* [7] *For there are three that bear witness in heaven: the Father, the Word, and the*

---

[8] *The Wisdom of the Hebrew Alphabet* by Michael L. Munk, p.71

Holy Spirit; and these three are one. ⁸ And there are three that bear witness on earth: the Spirit, the water, and the blood; and these three agree as one. ⁹ If we receive the witness of men, the witness of God is greater; for this is the witness of God which He has testified of His Son. ¹⁰ He who believes in the Son of God has the witness in himself; he who does not believe God has made Him a liar, because he has not believed the testimony that God has given of His Son [ALEF-TAV]. ¹¹ And this is the testimony: that God has given us eternal life, and this life is in His Son. ¹² He who has the Son has life; he who does not have the Son of God does not have life. ¹³ These things I have written to you who believe in the name of the Son of God, that you may know that you have eternal life, and that you may continue to believe in the name of the Son of God" (1 John 5:1-13 additions mine).

Since GIMEL (ג) is the third letter of the Hebrew Alphabet, it represents the three that bear witness in heaven—the Father, the Son, and the Holy Spirit (1 John 5:7). GIMEL (ג) also represents the three that bear witness on earth—the Spirit, the water, and the blood (1 John 5:8).

An interesting connection to the three that bear witness in heaven is when YHVH (יהוה) appeared to Abraham, the LORD revealed Himself as three men:

"Now the Lᴏʀᴅ [YHVH] appeared to Abraham by the oaks of Mamre, while he was sitting at the tent door in the heat of the day. ² When he raised his eyes and looked, behold, three men were standing opposite him; and when he saw them, he ran from the tent door to meet them and bowed down to the ground, ³ and said, 'My Lord, if now I have found favor in Your sight, please do not pass Your servant by' " (Genesis 18:1-3 NASB).

What is this perfect provision and nourishment of the "Kingdom of God" latent within GIMEL (ג)? Let's take a glimpse at the phrase "Kingdom of God" in Scripture to gain more understanding.

"Strengthening the souls of the disciples, exhorting them to continue in the faith, and saying, "We must through many tribulations enter the Kingdom of God" (Acts 14:22). Suffering is simply part of our crucifixion process that enables us to enter the death, burial, and resurrection life of the Kingdom of God. Nothing better develops Christ's character within us than distress, suffering, and tribulations.

" ¹²Beloved, do not think it strange concerning the fiery trial which is to try you, as though some strange thing happened to you; ¹³ but rejoice to the extent that you partake of Christ's sufferings, that when His glory is revealed, you may also be glad with exceeding joy" (1 Peter 4:12-13).

As we offer our sufferings and sacrifices to Him, we are crucified in union with Christ in an ever-increasing measure, so we can live by the faith of the Son of God (Gal. 2:20).

"I now rejoice in my sufferings for you, and fill up in my flesh what is lacking in the afflictions of Christ, for the sake of His body, which is the church" (Colossians 1:24).

The final and most difficult quantum step of faith is having the exact same faith OF Christ. It's where those made after the Order of Melchizedek are made into the image of the Son of God (Hebrews 7:3):

"I am crucified with Christ: nevertheless I live; yet not I, but Christ lives in me: and the life which I now live in the flesh I live by the <u>faith of the Son of God</u>, who loved me, and gave himself for me" (Galatians 2:20_{KJV}).

"Here is the patience of the saints; here are those who keep the commandments of God and the <u>faith of Jesus</u>" (Revelation 14:12).

Two chief characteristics of a son of God are that they serve God with a whole heart (1 Chr. 28:9) and keep God's commandments (Prov. 7:1-2; 1 John 2:3-6; Rev. 14:12). We are not talking about something yucky and legalistic, but a State of Being that resonates at the same frequency as ALEF-TAV (את).

Having a humble, teachable heart is a preeminent hallmark of a maturing or mature son of God (Prov. 2-7). Growing, maturing sons continually endeavor to work out their salvation with fear and trembling (Phil. 2:12), according to the righteous and just standards of God's throne (Psa. 89:14). Please be encouraged, because this is a divine work of sanctification that's done not by your might, nor your power, but by His Spirit (Zech. 4:6). All that God requires from you and I is that we put our best foot forward in obeying His Word and surrendering to His Spirit. Know that the Righteous Order of Melchizedek is the highest spiritual order on earth that manifests heaven—making the kingdoms of this earth, the kingdoms of our God (Rev. 11:15).

Scripturally, when we are born from above (born-again), we merely SEE the Kingdom of God according to John 3:3. We are immature sons at this point. Two verses later, John 3:5 tells us that when we are born of water and the Spirit, we ENTER the Kingdom of God. It is during this step that Manifested Sons, or the Maturing Sons, are produced. This is where the New Living Creature of the One New Man in Christ begins to take shape. In its fullness, there will be a company within the Order of Melchizedek who are Christ's having crucified their flesh. They are the ones that have truly earned the title—Crucified Ones. They are those who are led by the Spirit and INHERIT the Kingdom of God (Gal. 5:19-21; 1 Cor. 6:9-10). Inheriting the Kingdom of God is the third level, this is where Mature or Maturing Sons become His Pure and Spotless Bride—His Most Precious One.

Please refer to the *Quantum 22™: The Hebrew Living™ Letters* book for further revelation about GIMEL (ג) and the Biblical Series of Three.

Thoughts

The Way Of Wisdom

1. How can you practically seek first the Kingdom of God and His righteousness (Matt. 6:33) and why do you think these two elements are linked to God's provision?

_____

_____

_____

2. Dig a little deeper into the three that bear witness in heaven, the Father, the Word, and the Holy Spirit (1 John 5:7). First, personally connect to the Lord to set your heart to seek His truth, so you can flow by His Spirit when you look up Scriptures about:

"The Father" (John 5:19; Rom. 8:15; etc.):

_____

_____

_____

"The Word" (John 1:1; James 1:21; etc.):

_____

_____

_____

"The Holy Spirit" (John 14:26; Rom. 14:17; etc.):

_____

_____

_____

3. Dig a little deeper into the three that bear witness on earth that agree as one: the Spirit, the water, and the blood (1 John 5:8). First, personally connect to the Lord to set your heart to seek His truth, so you can flow by His Spirit when you look up Scriptures about:

"The Spirit" (Gen. 1:2; John 1:32; Eph. 2:22; etc.):

_____

_____

_____

"The water" (Psa. 42:1; Mark 1:10; John 4:14; etc.):

_____

_____

_____

"The blood" (Exo. 12:13; Eph. 2:13; Col. 1:20; etc.):

_____

_____

_____

4. What is the perfect provision and nourishment of the "Kingdom of God" latent within GIMEL (ג)? Research the phrase "Kingdom of God" in Scripture.

"The **Kingdom of God** is at hand; repent and believe in the gospel" (Mark 1:15).

_____

_____

_____

"The **Kingdom of God** is like a man who casts seed upon the soil" (Mark 4:26-32).

_____

_____

_____

"Whoever does not receive the **Kingdom of God** like a child will not enter it at all" (Mark 10:14-15).

_____

_____

_____

"How hard it will be for those who are wealthy to enter the **Kingdom of God!**" (Mark 10:23).

_____

_____

_____

"Blessed are you who are poor, for yours is the **Kingdom of God**" (Luke 6:20).

_____

_____

_____

*"And He sent them out to proclaim the **Kingdom of God** and to perform healing"* (Luke 9:2).

_____

_____

_____

*"But if I cast out the demons by the finger of God, then the **Kingdom of God** has come upon you"* (Luke 11:20).

_____

_____

_____

*"The **Kingdom of God** is not coming with signs that can be observed"* (Luke 17:20). Note: This coincides with the mustard seed parable.

_____

_____

_____

*"For behold, the **Kingdom of God** is in your midst [within you]"* (Luke 17:21).

_____

_____

_____

*"We must through many tribulations enter the **Kingdom of God**"* (Acts 14:22).

_____

_____

_____

5. Contemplate the three stages of seeing, entering, and inheriting the Kingdom of God (John 3:3; John 3:5; Mark 10:23-25; Acts 14:22; Gal. 5:19-21; 1 Cor. 6:9-10).

_____

_____

_____

_____

GIMEL (ג)

What is the most important ALEF-TAV (את) facet of wisdom in your eyes about GIMEL (ג)'s provision?

PRACTICE WRITING GIMEL

● Pronounced *geeh-mel* ●

Start at the top. Draw across to the right and then down to the baseline.
Second, draw the bottom left leg from the middle of the first line.

is the letter of bestowing lovingkindness—GIMILUT HASIDIM (גְּמִילוּת חֲסָדִים).
Loving kindness leaves an eternal mark upon the place that it's performed as well as elevating people to heavenly levels.

DALET

WISDOM SIX

ד
DALET

DALET (ד)

DALET (ד) is the fourth *Hebrew Living™ Letter* of the Alef-Bet. It is pronounced *dah-let*. DALET (ד) has the numerical value of 4, which means that the Hebrews use it for the number 4.

The ancient pictograph for DALET (ד) agrees with the meaning of its name. In ancient Hebrew DALET means a door, which symbolizes a door, a path or a way of life, and movement especially into or out of. [9]

DALET (ד) IN ALEF-TAV (את)

You and I can personally choose to engage the essence of Messiah Yeshua—the Word of God—contained within the Hebrew letter DALET (ד). Since the pictograph for the Hebrew letter DALET (ד) is a door, we travel to Yeshua's declarations about "I am the door."

> " 'Most assuredly, I say to you, he who does not enter the sheepfold by the door, but climbs up some other way, the same is a thief and a robber. [2] But he who enters by the door is the shepherd of the sheep. [3] To him the doorkeeper opens, and the sheep hear his voice; and he calls his own sheep by name and leads them out. [4] And when he brings out his own sheep, he goes before them; and the sheep follow him, for they know his voice. [5] Yet they will by no means follow a stranger, but will flee from him, for they do not know the voice of strangers.' [6] Jesus used this illustration, but they did not understand the things which He spoke to them. [7] Then Jesus said to them again, 'Most assuredly, I say to you, <u>I am the door</u> of the sheep. [8] All who ever came before Me are thieves and robbers, but the sheep did not hear them. [9] <u>I am the door</u>. If anyone enters by Me, he will be saved, and will go in and out and find pasture. [10] The thief does not come except to steal, and to kill, and to destroy. I have come that they may have life, and that they may have it more abundantly' "
> (John 10:1-10).

John 8:12 through John 10:42 portrays Yeshua's walk during the Feast of Dedication (i.e., Hanukkah). Significantly, Yeshua declares twice *"I am the door"* in the midst of God's Winter One-Dear-Land.

---

[9]*Hebrew Word Pictures* by Frank T. Seekins, Dalet, p. 24

DALET (ד) is 4. There are 13 references in Scripture to the "four living creatures" who have "four faces" each, "four sides" each, "four wings" each and a total of four wheels within wheels.

"Behold, the _four_ wheels by the cherubim, one wheel by one cherub" (Ezekiel 10:9).

The four wheels within wheels of the four living creatures have the appearance of beryl: *"The appearance of the wheels and their work was like unto the color of a _beryl_: and they _four_ had one likeness: and their appearance and their work was as it were a wheel in the middle of a wheel" (Ezekiel 1:16$_{KJV}$).* Beryl is the principal store of beryllium in the earth's crust. Notably, beryl crystals occur in hexagonal prisms—a polygon of six angles and six sides. The Star of David is an emblem consisting of two interlacing triangles forming a six-pointed star. When we connect the beryl wheels with a certain man dressed with a gold belt that had a body of beryl in Daniel 10:6, we can get a glimpse of the corporate body of Christ that has been stamped with the royal seal of the Messiah's Hebraic roots. DALET (ד) is the door to the corporate body of Christ quantumly flying by the Holy Spirit with one another.

The spirit of each of the four living creatures is in its wheels:

" ¹⁹ And when the living creatures went, the wheels went by them: and when the living creatures were lifted up from the earth, the wheels were lifted up. ²⁰ Whithersoever the spirit was to go, they went, thither was their spirit to go; and the wheels were lifted up over against them: for the spirit of the living creature was in the wheels. ²¹ When those went, these went; and when those stood, these stood; and when those were lifted up from the earth, the wheels were lifted up over against them: for the spirit of the living creature was in the wheels" (Ezekiel 1:19-21$_{KJV}$).

The spirit within each of the four whirling wheels has several applications. The first level of God's Chariot Throne is a personal one. A person (face of a man) must connect intimately in their fourfold unity with the Father (face of an ox), the Son (face of a lion), and the Holy Spirit (face of an eagle). Once they are firing on all cylinders to the best of their ability in oneness with God's perfect heart, a person's spirit locks into living and moving and having their being in Him (Acts 17:28). This is where the saying is true: "I am a wheel within His wheel created to do good works according to His perfect will."

I teach extensively about how the Cherubim in Scripture is a picture of the New Living Creature made after the Order of Melchizedek. *"This is the Living Creature I saw under the God of Israel by the river Chebar; and I knew that they were the cherubim" (Ezekiel 10:20$_{KJV}$).* When a righteous wing of God's Melchizedek Army (four or more believers who have entered the Kingdom of God) fly by the Spirit with one another, they rise through the Revelation 4:1 DOOR—Yeshua—to stand at the DOOR of the East Gate where Jesus returns to earth:

"For just as the lightning comes from the east and flashes even to the west, so will the coming of the Son of Man be" (Matthew 24:27$_{NASB}$).

Note: The "Son of Man" references in Scripture indicate where the sons of man (i.e., mankind) need to walk so that they can be made like unto the "Son of God."

"And the Cherubim lifted up their wings, and mounted up from the earth in my sight: when they went out, the wheels also were beside them, and every one stood at the door of the east gate of the Lord's House; and the glory of the God of Israel was over them above" (Ezekiel 10:19 KJV).

"After these things I looked and behold, a door standing open in heaven, and the first voice which I had heard, like the sound of a trumpet speaking with me, said, Come up here, and I will show you what must take place after these things. And immediately I was in the Spirit; and behold, a throne was standing in heaven, and One sitting on the throne" (Revelation 4:1-2 NASB).

Remember, we are supposed to walk like Yeshua (Jesus), talk like Yeshua, and be exactly like Yeshua. Also, remember Yeshua's declaration *"I am from above"* (John 8:23). The ultimate purpose of the Cherubim Classification of the Order of Melchizedek is to become the fully mature Body of the Messiah that holds fast to the Head—Messiah Yeshua. This is accomplished by the kings and priests of the Order of Melchizedek leading their own inner fire bride forth. Once we are manifestly wedded as the Bride of the Messiah, we then become incorporated into His Oneness Metatron Matrix (i.e., become completely one with Messiah Yeshua).

Esther 6:2 reveals that the king's chamberlains are the keepers of the DOOR. The king's chamberlains are the kings and priests of the Eternal Order of Melchizedek who are treasurers of the most intimate.

YHVH's Melchizedek Company is the predecessor for the unparalleled beauty of His Pure and Spotless Bridal Company. They both have pure hearts surrounded by Yeshua's Blood, which passes through the righteous judgments that emanate from His Sapphire Throne. Behold, the Judge stands at the DOOR (James 5:9).

One of the bridal preparation functions that the Order of Melchizedek operates in is the role of the king's chamberlain. A chamberlain is an attendant of a sovereign king in his bedchamber. He is the chief officer in the household of a king who is the treasurer of his most intimate possessions. Behold, *"My beloved put in his hand by the hole of the door, and my bowels were moved for him"* (Song of Songs 5:4 KJV).

As guardians of the king's most cherished treasures—our very selves and everyone made in His image—the royal priests of Melchizedek are in charge of receiving, keeping, and disbursing the king's resources according to His heart.

One of the primary doors that we are guardians of is the door of our own hearts. This is supposed to be the main focus of Hanukkah. The Messiah's Biblical Feast of Dedication is most importantly the dedication of one's own heart.

It's a major deal that a DOOR/GATE is mentioned for each one of the four abominations listed in Ezekiel chapter 8. These four detestable things drive God far from His sanctuary—His Dwelling Presence (Ezekiel 8:5,7-8,14,16). These four abominations map to the four faces of God (the four faces of Melchizedek) listed as follows: *"As for the likeness of their faces, each had the face of a man; each of the four had the face of a lion on the right side, each of the four had the face of an ox on the left side, and each of the four had the face of an eagle"* (Ezekiel 1:10). To the degree that we compromise with the four abominations is the degree that we do not operate in the fullness of the Order of Melchizedek. This means that we will not be completely ruling and reigning in Christ in those compromised areas. For much more on this subject, check out the book: *SANTA-TIZING: What's wrong with Christmas and how to clean it up* book. [10]

---

[10]*SANTA-TIZING: What's wrong with Christmas and how to clean it up* by Robin Main. https://www.amazon.com/SANTA-TIZING-Whats-wrong-Christmas-clean/dp/1607911159/

The Way Of Wisdom

1. The "Son of Man" references in Scripture indicate where the sons of man (mankind) need to walk so that they can be made like unto the "Son of God." Delve into some of the Scriptural references for "Son of Man" to pull out the gold pavement where believers need to walk.

The **Son of Man** is the part of the Body of Christ that seeks to attach firmly to the Head (Matt. 8:20; Eph. 4:15-16; Col. 2:19).

_____

_____

_____

The **Son of Man** has the power to forgive sins on earth (Matt. 9:6, Mark 2:10). Note: The Bible teaches if you want your heavenly Father to forgive you, you must forgive people their trespasses against you (Matt. 6:14-15).

_____

_____

_____

The **Son of Man** is the Lord of the Sabbath (Matt. 12:8, Mark 2:28). Contemplate and apply the ascended reality that He is your Sabbath Rest and you are His (Heb. 4:9-12).

_____

_____

_____

The person who sows the good seed is the **Son of Man** (Matt. 13:37). Contemplate that if one understands the Parable of the Sower, they understand all parables (Mark 4:13).

_____

_____

_____

The **Son of Man** is risen from the dead (Matt. 17:9, Mark 9:9). Additionally, the **Son of Man** was three days and three nights in the heart of the earth (Matt. 12:40).

_____

_____

_____

The **Son of Man** is betrayed into the hands of men (Matt. 17:22; Mark 14:41).

_____

_____

_____

As the days of Noah were, so will be the coming of the **Son of Man** (Matt. 24:37).

_____

_____

_____

The **Son of Man** suffers many things (Mark 8:31).

_____

_____

_____

The **Son of Man** came to serve and give His life a ransom for many (Mark 10:45).

_____

_____

_____

The **Son of Man** is glorified (John 13:31).

_____

_____

_____

2. Why is ALEF-TAV (את) the DALET (ד) door to people becoming united in the Body of Christ? Hint: Ephesians 5:23 and Colossians 1:18.

_____

_____

_____

_____

_____

3. What are the major components of God's Chariot Throne—*Merkabah*—shown in Ezckiel 1 and Ezekiel 10? Ask for His spirit of understanding and enlightenment as you study.

"Whirlwind" (Ezek. 1:4).

_____

_____

_____

"Fire" (Ezek. 1:4,13; Ezek. 10:2,7).

_____

_____

_____

"Four living creatures" (Ezek. 1:5).

_____

_____

_____

"Likeness of a man" (Ezek. 1:5).

_____

_____

_____

"Four faces" each—lion, ox, eagle, and man (Ezek. 1:6,8; Ezek. 10:14).

_____

_____

_____

"Four wings" each (Ezek. 1:6,8).

_____

_____

_____

A man's hand under their wings (Ezek. 1:8; Ezek. 10:8).

_____

_____

_____

Beryl looking wheel within a wheel beside each living creature (Ezek. 1:15-16; Ezek. 10:9).

_____

_____

_____

Firmament upon the heads of the Corporate New Living Creature (Ezek. 1:22; Ezek. 10:1).

_____

_____

_____

Voice of the Almighty (Ezek. 1:24; Ezek. 10:5).

_____

_____

_____

A man upon a sapphire throne (Ezek. 1:26; Ezek. 10:1).

_____

_____

_____

Rainbow-colored glory of YHVH is above the Chariot Throne (Ezek. 1:28; Ezek. 10:4,18-19).

_____

_____

_____

The Corporate New Living Creature made up of four or more living creatures is the Cherubim (Ezek. 10:20).

_____

_____

_____

DALET (ד)

What new ALEF-TAV (את) aspect of wisdom have you learned about His DALET (ד) door?

PRACTICE WRITING DALET

● Pronounced *dah-let* ●

Start at the left to draw the top horizontal line.

Then, draw the vertical line to the right from the top horizontal line to the bottom line.

ד

is the door for His sheep. On the
night when God brought out His
people from Egypt (the world)
with a mighty hand and
outstretched arm, they were
instructed to put the blood
DAHM (דָּם) of the Passover
Lamb on their door
DELET (דֶּלֶת),
which represented entrance to
the home of their heart.

HEI

WISDOM SEVEN

ה
HEI

HEI/HEY/HE (ה)

HEI (ה) is the fifth *Hebrew Living™ Letter* of the Alef-Bet. It is pronounced *hey*. HEI (ה) has the numerical value of 5, which means that the Hebrews use it for the number 5.

The ancient pictograph for HEI (ה) agrees with the meaning of its name. In ancient Hebrew HEI means behold. HEI's pictograph is a picture of a man with his hands lifted up, or of an open window over a man's head. HEI (ה)'s window symbolizes behold, to show, and to reveal. [11]

HEI (ה) IN ALEF-TAV (את)

You and I can personally choose to engage the essence of Messiah Yeshua—the Word of God—contained within the Hebrew letter HEI (ה). Behold, there are many names for God. He is called The Almighty, The Omnipresent, The Omniscient, etc. These names are based on various attributes of God and how He makes Himself known to us. However, the four-letter name YHVH is different. It is more of a personal name than an adjective. The most common name for God in scripture is YHVH (יהוה). This Name is derived from the verb *lihiyot* להיות, which means "to be."

Notice the double portion of HEIs (ה) in YHVH (יהוה). YHVH is called the Ineffable Name or the Unspeakable Name of God. Due to YHVH being composed of four Hebrew letters—YUD, HEI, VAV, HEI—it is also referred to as the Tetragrammaton, which literally means "the four letters." It is a combination of *'ha-ya'* היה (was) *'ho-ve'* הוה (is) and *'ye-he-ye'* יהיה (will be) together, and it symbolizes the timeless nature of God who was, who is and who always will be in existence.

YHVH (י-ה-ו-ה) is the Name that represents God as the Eternal for its four Hebrew letters form the words *"He was, He is, He will be."* When Moses encountered God at the burning bush, Moses asked: "What is your name?" Moses was told: אהיה אשר אהיה –*ehyeh asher ehyeh* *"I will be what I will be"* or *"I am that I am" (Exodus 3:14).*

Let's dive a little deeper into the phrase *ehyeh asher ehyeh*, which is derived from the Qal imperfect first person form of the Hebrew verb *lihiyot*—"I will be." YHVH is the source of all being. He has a transcendence State of Being. So, our understanding of *lihiyot* can be simplified into a righteous State of Being that resonates at the same frequency in which it was originally created. Just as His creation began with His command *"Let there be light,"* so will His Kingdom. God wants everything to be redeemed and restored to the pristine state that He originally created. He wants us to go back to Eden and beyond.

---

[11] *Hebrew Word Pictures* by Frank T. Seekins, Hey, p. 28

My son minored in Hebrew in college. He told me that *lihiyot* is a unique verb. The *Hayah* verb tense of *lihiyot* carries meaning in the past of what was done. *Hayah* carries a meaning in the future of what will be done, but a present tense does not exist for this verb. Instead, it is given that the verb "to be" is just there. The present (i.e., presence) tense of *hayah* is who you are, like "I Robin." The "am" in "I am Robin" is already understood to exist, and it manifests in what a person is actually doing. This is our present reality or state of being.

In Exodus Chapter 6, God instructs Moses to go to the children of Israel and tell them:

> *"I am YHVH. I appeared to Abraham, to Isaac, and to Jacob with [the name] El Shaddai, but [with] My name YHVH, I did not become known to them" (Exodus 6:3).*

Elijah found out that the barely heard (ה) alludes to God. Elijah experienced a strong wind that rent the mountains and shattered the rocks. He experienced an earthquake and a fire, but the Lord was not present in any of these violent phenomena. Then *"after the fire was a soundless whisper, and in it appeared God" (1 Kings 19:12).*

Did you know that Hebrew history records that the letter HEI (ה) was attached to the Ark of His Presence? The Holy Ark of the Covenant was enveloped in a ה-shaped cloud—when it preceded the Israelites during their wilderness travels. The ה-shaped cloud was a visible sign of God's special guidance and presence. [12] As it is written, *"and HASHEM would go before them by day in a pillar of cloud to lead them on the way" (Exodus 13:21).*

Around a thousand years later, Nehemiah stood in Jerusalem inspiring the Israelites to repent. To underline God's incredible and continuous care for His people in the wilderness, Nehemiah paraphrased Exodus 13:21 by adding a HEI (ה), which emphasized that it was God who led them (Midrash Aggadah 2:79). [13]

> *" [17] They refused to obey, And they were not mindful of Your wonders That You did among them. But they hardened their necks, And in their rebellion they appointed a leader to return to their bondage. But You are God, Ready to pardon, Gracious and merciful, Slow to anger, Abundant in kindness, And did not forsake them. [18] Even when they made a molded calf for themselves, And said, 'This is your god That brought you up out of Egypt,' And worked great provocations, [19] Yet in Your manifold mercies You did not forsake them in the wilderness. The pillar of the cloud did not depart from them by day, To lead them on the road; Nor the pillar of fire by night, To show them light, And the way they should go" (Nehemiah 9:17-19).*

---

[12] *The Wisdom of the Hebrew Alphabet* by Rabbi Michael L. Munk, p. 88
[13] *The Wisdom of the Hebrew Alphabet* by Rabbi Michael L. Munk, p. 88

Thoughts

The Way Of Wisdom

1. What is your current *hayah* state of being? Recall that the Hebrew verb for "I will be" is a unique verb. *Hayah* carries meaning in the past of what was done. *Hayah* carries meaning in the future of what will be done, but its present tense does not exist. This is because the present tense of *hayah* is already understood to exist, and it is displayed through what a person is doing. In the present, *Hayah* is your current state of being. Behold, I am that I am.

_____

_____

_____

_____

_____

2. What are your thoughts about the double portion of HEIs (ה) in YHVH (יהוה)? Remember that the four-letter name YHVH (יהוה) is different because it is more of a personal name than an adjective and it's the most common name for God in Scripture. Also, don't forget that YHVH (יהוה) derives from the verb להיות, which means "to be."

_____

_____

_____

_____

_____

3. Research various occurrences of "behold" in the first five books of the Bible (Torah). Get a "feel" for what it means when the term "behold" is used in the Bible, make note of common themes that go with "behold", and its range of connections to "I am." For instance:

*"Then the LORD God said, '**Behold**, the man has become like one of Us, to know good and evil"* (Genesis 3:22).

_____

_____

_____

*"And **behold**, the word of the LORD came to him"* (Genesis 15:4).

_____

_____

_____

*"And it came to pass, when the sun went down and it was dark, that **behold**, there appeared a smoking oven and a burning torch that passed between those pieces" (Genesis 15:17).*

_____

_____

_____

*"As for Me, **behold**, My covenant is with you, and you shall be a father of many nation" (Genesis 17:4).*

_____

_____

_____

*"Then the LORD [YHVH] appeared to him by the terebinth trees of Mamre, as he was sitting in the tent door in the heat of the day. So he lifted his eyes and looked, and **behold**, three men were standing by him" (Genesis 18:1-2).*

_____

_____

_____

*"Then he dreamed, and **behold**, a ladder was set up on the earth, and its top reached to heaven; and there the angels of God were ascending and descending on it" (Genesis 28:12).*

_____

_____

_____

*"And **behold**, the LORD stood above it and said: **"I am the LORD God of Abraham your father and the God of Isaac; the land on which you lie I will give to you and your descendants"** (Genesis 28:13).*

_____

_____

_____

*"**Behold, I am with you** and will keep you wherever you go, and will bring you back to this land; for I will not leave you until I have done what I have spoken to you" (Genesis 28:15).*

_____

_____

_____

*"And the Angel of the LORD appeared to him in a flame of fire from the midst of a bush. So he looked, and **behold**, the bush was burning with fire, but the bush was not consumed" (Exodus 3:2).*

_____

_____

_____

*"Then the LORD said to Moses, "**Behold**, I will rain bread from heaven for you. And the people shall go out and gather a certain quota every day, that I may test them, whether they will walk in My law or not" (Exodus 16:4).*

_____

_____

_____

*"Now it came to pass, as Aaron spoke to the whole congregation of the children of Israel, that they looked toward the wilderness, and **behold**, the glory of the LORD appeared in the cloud" (Exodus 16:10).*

_____

_____

_____

*"And the LORD said to Moses, '**Behold**, I come to you in the thick cloud, that the people may hear when I speak with you, and believe you forever' " (Exodus 19:9).*

_____

_____

_____

*"**Behold**, I send an Angel before you to keep you in the way and to bring you into the place which I have prepared" (Exodus 23:20).*

_____

_____

_____

*"**Behold**, I set before you today a blessing and a curse" (Deuteronomy 11:26).*

_____

_____

_____

4. Sit with the Lord and ask Him to speak to you about how He revealed Himself to Moses was told: אהיה אשר אהיה–*ehyeh asher ehyeh* *"I will be what I will be"* or *"I am that I am"* (*Exodus 3:14*).

_____

_____

_____

_____

5. How can you apply to your own life the concept of a ה-shaped cloud enveloping the Ark of the Covenant in the Wilderness when it preceded the Israelites in their travels? Recall the ה-shaped cloud was a visible sign of God's special guidance and protection (Exo. 13:21).

_____

_____

_____

_____

6. Look up how "behold" is used in the book of Job. Notice how it highlights concise and profound truths:

*"**Behold**, happy is the man whom God corrects; Therefore do not despise the chastening of the Almighty"* (*Job 5:17*).

_____

_____

_____

*"**Behold**, this is the joy of His way, And out of the earth others will grow. **Behold**, God will not cast away the blameless, Nor will He uphold the evildoers"* (*Job 8:19-20*).

_____

_____

_____

*"And to man He said, '**Behold**, the fear of the Lord, that is wisdom, And to depart from evil is understanding'"* (*Job 28:28*).

_____

_____

_____

7. Look up how King David used "behold" in the book of Psalms. What are your views on why he emphasized these thoughts with "behold."?

*"**Behold**, the wicked brings forth iniquity; Yes, he conceives trouble and brings forth falsehood"* (Psalms 7:14).

_____

_____

_____

_____

*"The LORD is in His holy temple, The LORD's throne is in heaven; His eyes **behold**, His eyelids test the sons of men. . . . For the LORD is righteous, He loves righteousness; His countenance **behold**s the upright"* (Psalms 11:4, 7).

_____

_____

_____

_____

*"**Behold**, the eye of the LORD is on those who fear Him, On those who hope in His mercy"* (Psalms 33:18).

_____

_____

_____

*"Then I said, '**Behold**, I come; In the scroll of the book it is written of me'"* (Psalms 40:7).

_____

_____

_____

*"**Behold**, I long for Your precepts; Revive me in Your righteousness"* (Psalms 119:40).

_____

_____

_____

HEI (ה)

What ALEF-TAV (את) way of wisdom regarding the Hebrew letter HEI (ה) is most insightful for you?

PRACTICE WRITING HEI

● Pronounced *hey* ●

Start at the top at the short line on the left. Draw straight down to the bottom line. This is an inverted YUD (׳). Then, reposition your pen with the proper spacing above the short line to draw the DALET (ד), which is the top horizontal line that connects with a sharp corner to the vertical line on the right.

is the letter of the most effortless
sound a soul can make . . . taking
a breath. That is why there is
some of ה in every word and why
it seems so unfathomable for it is
the sound of being present—
HAYAH (הָיָה). Hey!
God says to each of us:
EHYEH ASHER EHYEH
(אֶהְיֶה אֲשֶׁר אֶהְיֶה)
"I will be what I will be"
(Exo. 3:14). Not who you want
me to be. To be is to exist,
to abide, to remain, to continue,
to accompany, and to occur.

WISDOM EIGHT

ו
VAV

VAV / WAW (ו)

VAV (ו) is the sixth *Hebrew Living™ Letter* of the Alef-Bet. It is pronounced *vahv*. VAV (ו) has the numerical value of 6, which means that the Hebrews use it for the number 6.

The ancient pictograph for VAV (ו) agrees with the meaning of its name. In ancient Hebrew VAV means a nail, wooden peg, or hook which symbolizes joining together, making secure, and becoming bound. [14]

VAV (ו) IN ALEF-TAV (את)

You and I can personally choose to engage the essence of Messiah Yeshua—the Word of God—contained within the Hebrew letter VAV (ו). The first VAV (ו) in God's Word is in *Genesis 1:1*—*"In the beginning God created the heavens and* [VAV] *the earth."* This first VAV (ו) in Scripture sets precedence. It's the sixth Hebrew word as well as the twenty-second letter of the first verse. Thus, this first VAV alludes to the power to connect all the powers of the Hebrew letters from ALEF (א) to TAV (ת).

Hebrew Mystics reveal that in the beginning of creation when infinite light filled all-in-all (i.e., all reality), God contracted His Infinite Light to create a place—a hollow empty space as it were—for the existence of finite worlds. Into this "vacuum," God figuratively drew down a single line of light from the Infinite Source. Behold, through ALEF-TAV (את), who is the Light of the World, all things came to be and are constantly upheld through the word of His power (i.e., the power of the word). The essential creative essences for our world that are resident in Messiah Yeshua are the Hebrew letters through which He upholds all things—the very fiber of your being.

> *" ¹ God, who at various times and in various ways spoke in time past to the fathers by the prophets, ² has in these last days spoken to us by His Son, whom He has appointed heir of all things, through whom also He made the worlds; ³ who being the brightness of His glory and the express image of His person, and upholding all things by the word of His power, when He had by Himself purged our sins, sat down at the right hand of the Majesty on high, ⁴ having become so much better than the angels, as He has by inheritance obtained a more excellent name than they" (Hebrews 1:1-4).*

---

[14] *Hebrew Word Pictures* by Frank T. Seekins, Vav, p. 32

These Hebrew Sages say that this single ray of light is the secret of the Hebrew letter VAV (ו). The first VAV in the Bible serves to join matter (this spacetime continuum) with spirit (eternity). The first VAV shows us ALEF-TAV and His power to connect heaven and earth. The mature Body of Christ (Messiah) will walk in this crossover place too, bringing heaven to earth.

It is always wise to be humble and teachable; because in this Kingdom Day, the royal priests of the Order of Melchizedek will come in the Spirit of Elijah to restore all things: *"Jesus answered and said to them, 'Indeed, Elijah is coming first and will restore all things' " (Matthew 17:11).*

> *"Repent therefore and be converted, that your sins may be blotted out, so that times of refreshing may come from the presence of the Lord, and that He may send Jesus Christ, who was preached to you before, whom heaven must receive until the times of the restoration of all things, which God has spoken by the mouth of all His holy prophets since the world began" (Acts 3:19-21).*

> *" 'For behold, the day is coming, Burning like an oven, And all the proud, yes, all who do wickedly will be stubble. And the day which is coming shall burn them up,' Says the Lord of hosts, 'That will leave them neither root nor branch. ² But to you who fear My name The Sun of Righteousness shall arise with healing in His wings; And you shall go out and grow fat like stall-fed calves. ³ You shall trample the wicked, For they shall be ashes under the soles of your feet on the day that I do this,' Says the Lord of hosts. ⁴ 'Remember the Law of Moses, My servant, Which I commanded him in Horeb for all Israel, With the statutes and judgments. ⁵ Behold, I will send you Elijah the prophet Before the coming of the great and dreadful day of the Lord. ⁶ And he will turn the hearts of the fathers to the children, And the hearts of the children to their fathers, Lest I come and strike the earth with a curse' " (Malachi 4:1-6).*

We must always have an eye for redemption in everything, including some things that are associated with the Antichrist. Didn't God say that He is going to restore ALL things?

There is a missing ingredient for many believers these days. Mixture grieves God's heart, and He is NOT going to redeem anything whose origins are demonic or evil. The redemption of demonic and evil things is them being judged, no longer existing, and us returning to our pristine primordial state that resonates at the same frequency as the Word of God. *"But strong meat belongs to them that are of full age, even those who by reason of use have their senses exercised to discern both good and evil" (Hebrews 5:14).*

> *"Let love be without hypocrisy. Abhor what is evil. Cling to what is good" (Romans 12:9).*

The Antichrist's number is infamously 666. Because man was created in God's image on the sixth day, the number "6" is also the number of man. On a personal level, the Antichrist can be likened to a completely selfish man; but what is the Antichrist's goal? To become like God. To become the head of the body of the Messiah himself.

When *Revelation 13:18* says, *"Here is wisdom. Let him who has understanding calculate the number of the beast, for it is the number of a man: His number is 666,"* we need to examine the redemptive side of His double-edged sword. Just as one side of the double-edged sword for *"love covers a multitude of sins"* speaks of confidentiality while the other side speaks of us covering the sins we love, so it is with *"let him who has understanding calculate the number . . . 666."*

One side of the double-edged sword's understanding of "666" is that we know it is the number of the Antichrist Beast. The other side of "666" is the mystery of the number 666, which can also represent complete light—the Messiah Himself—when what the Antichrist has twisted is turned right side up. Let him who has understanding, behold, that "666" can additionally represent the redemption of the Messiah bodily (i.e., you and I).

"666" can either represent the darkness of a completely selfish man in our body soul, and spirit; or it can represent the complete transformation/transfiguration of our body, soul, and spirit into light . . . into the exact same image as Messiah. Let him who has understanding behold the redemption of all things. Let us behold (be and hold onto), I am the Light of the World! *Then Jesus spoke to them again, saying, 'I AM the Light of the World. He who follows Me shall not walk in darkness, but have the light of life' " (John 8:12).*

> *"As long as I AM in the world, I AM the Light of the World" (John 9:5).*
>
> *"You are the light of the world. A city set on a hill cannot be hidden; nor does anyone light a lamp and put it under a basket, but on the lampstand, and it gives light to all who are in the house. Let your light shine before men in such a way that they may see your good works, and glorify your Father who is in heaven" (Matthew 5:14-16 NASB).*

Recall that the pictograph for VAV (ו) symbolizes joining together, making secure, or becoming bound (nailed). Each Hebrew word has a primary root. The Hebrew letter VAV (ו) is unique in the Hebrew language in that there is only one Hebrew word whose root begins with this letter. This word is (וו)—hooks—as in the Wilderness Tabernacle's hooks on the pillars (Exo. 38:10). The Hebrew sage Radak explains: "These were pegs that protruded from the pillars, in the shape of a letter ו; they were used to hang the carcasses of the sacrifices when they were being skinned." (Sefer HaShorashim).

> *"All sins forgiven, the slate wiped clean, that old arrest warrant canceled and <u>nailed</u> to Christ's cross. He stripped all the spiritual tyrants in the universe of their sham authority at the Cross and marched them naked through the streets" (Colossians 2:14-15 MSG).*
>
> *"So the other disciples were saying to him, 'We have seen the Lord!' But he said to them, "Unless I see in His hands the imprint of the <u>nails</u>, and put my finger into the place of the <u>nails</u>, and put my hand into His side, I will not believe" (John 20:25 NASB).*

One of the mysteries of the three nails, which were used to crucify Yeshua, is the redemption of "666" because VAV is a picture of a nail and its numerical value is six. We can literally see the picture on the Cross that He redeemed the three nails: VAV-VAV-VAV.

Observe another mystery, the pictures of the first letters of the Hebrew words on the sign that hung on the Cross above Messiah Yeshua proclaimed: Behold, salvation comes by the nailed hand.

> *"Now Pilate wrote a title and put it on the cross. And the writing was: JESUS OF NAZARETH, THE KING OF THE JEWS. 20 Then many of the Jews read this title, for the place where Jesus was crucified was near the city; and it was written in Hebrew, Greek, and Latin. 21 Therefore the chief priests of the Jews said to Pilate, 'Do not write, "The King of the Jews," but, 'He said, "I am the King of the Jews.' " 22 Pilate answered, 'What I have written, I have written'" (John 19:19-22).*

The Way Of Wisdom

1. What is the secret of the Hebrew letter VAV (ו) and what makes it vital to our existence?

   _____

   _____

   _____

   _____

2. Study the Spirit of Elijah and the restoration of all things in Scripture.

   Malachi 4:5-6.

   _____

   _____

   _____

   Matthew 17:11.

   _____

   _____

   _____

   Mark 9:11-12.

   _____

   _____

   _____

   Acts 3:19-21.

   _____

   _____

   _____

3. Why do you think there is only one Hebrew root word in Scripture that begins with the letter VAV (ו)? Recall, this word is (וו)—hooks—as in the Wilderness Tabernacle's hooks on the pillars (Exodus 38:10). And why do you think that the Messiah's redemption of the picture of nails in the Tabernacle is so important?

   _____

   _____

   _____

4. Look up Scriptures that contain the word "nail" and add that to your Holy Spirit inspired revelation of Christ's three-nail redemption of the Antichrist's number 666.

*"David prepared iron in abundance for the **nail**s of the doors of the gates and for the joints" (1 Chr. 22:3).*

_____

_____

_____

*"The words of scholars are like well-driven **nail**s, given by one Shepherd" (Eccl. 12:11).*

_____

_____

_____

*"Now Thomas, called the Twin, one of the twelve, was not with them when Jesus came. ²⁵ The other disciples therefore said to him, 'We have seen the Lord.' So he said to them, 'Unless I see in His hands the print of the **nail**s, and put my finger into the print of the **nail**s, and put my hand into His side, I will not believe' " (John 20:24-25).*

_____

_____

_____

*"Having wiped out the handwriting of requirements that was against us, which was contrary to us. And He has taken it out of the way, having **nail**ed it to the cross" (Col. 2:14).*

_____

_____

_____

_____

5. The first VAV (ו) in the Bible shows us ALEF-TAV's power to connect heaven and earth. Research the phrase "heaven and earth." What understanding have you gained?

*"In the beginning God created the **heaven**s **and** the **earth**" (Gen. 1:1).*

_____

_____

_____

_____

*"This is the history of the **heavens and** the **earth** when they were created, in the day that the LORD God made the **earth and** the **heavens**" (Gen. 2:4).*

_____

_____

_____

_____

"Then Melchizedek king of Salem brought out bread and wine; he was the priest of God Most High.
*¹⁹ And he blessed him and said: 'Blessed be Abram of God Most High, Possessor of **heaven and earth**'"*
(Gen. 14:18-19).

_____

_____

_____

_____

*"I call **heaven and earth** as witnesses today against you, that I have set before you life and death, blessing and cursing; therefore choose life, that both you and your descendants may live" (Deut. 30:19).*

_____

_____

_____

_____

*"Yours, O LORD, is the greatness, The power and the glory, The victory and the majesty; For all that is in **heaven and** in **earth** is Yours; Yours is the kingdom, O LORD, And You are exalted as head over all"*
(1 Chr. 29:11).

_____

_____

_____

_____

*"Let **heaven and earth** praise Him, The seas and everything that moves in them" (Psalms 69:34).*

_____

_____

_____

_____

*"May you be blessed by the LORD, Who made **heaven and earth**"* (Psalms 115:15).

_____

_____

_____

*"My help comes from the LORD [YHVH], Who made **heaven and earth**"* (Psalms 121:2).

_____

_____

_____

*"The LORD also will roar from Zion, And utter His voice from Jerusalem; The **heavens and earth** will shake; But the LORD will be a shelter for His people, And the strength of the children of Israel"* (Joel 3:16).

_____

_____

_____

*"**Heaven and earth** will pass away, but My words will by no means pass away"* (Mark 13:31).

_____

_____

_____

*"For this reason I bow my knees to the Father of our Lord Jesus Christ, ¹⁵ from whom the whole family in **heaven and earth** is named, ¹⁶ that He would grant you, according to the riches of His glory, to be strengthened with might through His Spirit in the inner man, ¹⁷ that Christ may dwell in your hearts through faith; that you, being rooted and grounded in love, ¹⁸ may be able to comprehend with all the saints what is the width and length and depth and height— ¹⁹ to know the love of Christ which passes knowledge; that you may be filled with all the "fullness of God" (Eph. 3:14-19)."*

_____

_____

_____

_____

VAV (ו)

Which ALEF-TAV (את) feature of the wisdom of VAV (ו) has the utmost impact for you?

PRACTICE WRITING VAV

🔹 Pronounced *vahv* 🔹

Start to the left at the top. Make a short down sloping line toward your right;
then draw a line straight down to the bottom line.

וֹ

is the sound of being joined;
because it is the sound of the
word "and." Behold, God created
the heavens וֹ the earth. One can
only join another if they are both
distinct; otherwise, one would
absorb the other. This is not the
way of unity. The work of VAV
is to join us all into a myriad of
constellations where we each
remain unique,
yet we are bound to each other
being one in Christ.

WISDOM NINE

ז

ZAYIN

ZAYIN (ז)

ZAYIN (ז) is the seventh *Hebrew Living™ Letter* of the Alef-Bet that's pronounced *ZAH-yeen*. ZAYIN (ז) has the numerical value of 7, which means that the Hebrews use it for the number 7.

The ancient pictograph for ZAYIN (ז) agrees with the meaning of its name. In ancient Hebrew ZAYIN means a weapon and its pictograph looks like an axe or a sword. It symbolizes cutting or piercing. [15]

ZAYIN (ז) IN ALEF-TAV (את)

You and I can personally choose to engage the essence of Messiah Yeshua—the Word of God—contained within the Hebrew letter ZAYIN (ז). ZAYIN (ז) is a picture of a sword; therefore, the most direct ALEF-TAV (את) redemption for this Hebrew letter has to do with the living and active two-edged sword, which is the Word of God:

> "*14 Stand therefore, having girded your waist with truth, having put on the breastplate of righteousness, 15 and having shod your feet with the preparation of the gospel of peace; 16 above all, taking the shield of faith with which you will be able to quench all the fiery darts of the wicked one. 17 And take the helmet of salvation, and the sword of the Spirit, which is the word of God*" (Ephesians 6:14-17).

There is an incredible reality to the Word of God being living, active, and powerful.

> "*9 There remains therefore a rest for the people of God. 10 For he who has entered His rest has himself also ceased from his works as God did from His. 11 Let us therefore be diligent to enter that rest, lest anyone fall according to the same example of disobedience. 12 For the word of God is living and powerful, and sharper than any two-edged sword, piercing even to the division of soul and spirit, and of joints and marrow, and is a discerner of the thoughts and intents of the heart*" (Hebrews 4:9-12).

Notice how the impressive Word of God is the foundation of God's seventh-day rest.

---

[15]*Hebrew Word Pictures* by Frank T. Seekins, Zayin, p. 36

The chapter that begins with *"The Revelation of Jesus Christ, which God gave Him to show His servants"* *(Revelation 1:1)* reveals Messiah Yeshua both as the ALEF and TAV (תא) as well as having a sharp two-edged sword coming out of His mouth. Also, notice that the ZAYIN (ז) number "seven" is mentioned four times.

> *"¹⁰ I was in the Spirit on the Lord's Day [7ᵗʰ day], and I heard behind me a loud voice, as of a trumpet, ¹¹ saying, 'I am the Alpha [ALEF] and the Omega [TAV], the First and the Last,' and, 'What you see, write in a book and send it to the <u>seven</u> churches which are in Asia: to Ephesus, to Smyrna, to Pergamos, to Thyatira, to Sardis, to Philadelphia, and to Laodicea.' ¹² Then I turned to see the voice that spoke with me. And having turned I saw <u>seven</u> golden lampstands, ¹³ And in the midst of the <u>seven</u> lampstands One like the Son of Man, clothed with a garment down to the feet and girded about the chest with a golden band. ¹⁴ His head and hair were white like wool, as white as snow, and His eyes like a flame of fire; ¹⁵ His feet were like fine brass, as if refined in a furnace, and His voice as the sound of many waters; ¹⁶ He had in His right hand <u>seven</u> stars, <u>out of His mouth went a sharp two-edged sword</u>, and His countenance was like the sun shining in its strength"* *(Revelation 1:10-16 Additions mine).*

No wonder our incredibly delightful Messiah Yeshua is called "The Word of God"

> *"¹¹ Now I saw heaven opened, and behold [HEI], a white horse. And He who sat on him was called Faithful and True, and in righteousness He judges and makes war. ¹² His eyes [AYIN] were like a flame of fire, and on His head [RESH] were many crowns. He had a name written that no one knew except Himself. ¹³ He was clothed with a robe dipped in blood, and <u>His name is called The Word of God [ZAYIN]</u>. ¹⁴ And the armies in heaven, clothed in fine linen, white and clean, followed Him on white horses. ¹⁵ Now out of His mouth goes a sharp sword [ZAYIN], that with it He should strike the nations. And He Himself will rule them with a rod of iron. He Himself treads the winepress of the fierceness and wrath of Almighty God [SHIN]. ¹⁶ And He has on His robe and on His thigh a name written: KING OF KINGS AND LORD OF LORDS"* *(Revelation 19:11-16 Additions mine).*

The One called the Word of God that has a sharp sword coming out of His mouth is the King of Kings and Lord of Lords. Understandably, some extrapolate that the ALEF-TAV (את) word picture for the Hebrew letter ZAYIN (ז) can also be a scepter. ZAYIN (ז) has three small crown-like extensions *(tagim)* on top, and it is often referred to as the Golden Scepter שרבית הזהב of the King.

Thoughts

The Bible has seven declarations of Yeshua (Jesus) as king.

[1] First are the Wise Men who asked: *"Where is He who has been born King of the Jews?"* (Matthew 2:2). The sign above Yeshua's head on the Cross also declared Him as King: *"Jesus the King of the Jews"* (Matthew 27:37).

[2] Second, Yeshua taught that Jerusalem is the city of the great king: *"Jerusalem, the city of the great King"* (Matthew 5:35).

[3] Third, Yeshua was declared to be the King of Israel three times:

1. *"Let the Christ, the King of Israel, descend now from the cross, that we may see and believe"* (Mark 15:32).

2. *"Rabbi, You are the Son of God! You are the King of Israel!"* (John 1:49).

3. *"The next day a great multitude that had come to the feast, when they heard that Jesus was coming to Jerusalem, 13 took branches of palm trees and went out to meet Him, and cried out: 'Hosanna! "Blessed is He who comes in the name of the Lord!" The King of Israel!'"* (John 12:12-13).

[4] Fourth, the Apostle Paul wrote to Timothy: *"14 And the grace of our Lord was exceedingly abundant, with faith and love which are in Christ Jesus. 15 This is a faithful saying and worthy of all acceptance, that Christ Jesus came into the world to save sinners, of whom I am chief. . . . 17 Now to the King eternal, immortal, invisible, to God who alone is wise, be honor and glory forever and ever. Amen"* (1 Timothy 1:14-17).

[5] Fifth, in the Book of Hebrews, Yeshua is declared to be *"according to the Order of Melchizedek, a priest forever"* (Hebrews 4:5-6) and *"king of righteousness and king of peace"* (Hebrews 7:1-3).

[6] Sixth, in the Book of Revelation, Yeshua is presented as *"King of the nations"* (Revelation 15:3).

[7] Seventh, Yeshua is called by His majestic title *"King of Kings and Lord of Lords"* (Revelation 19:16).

There are seven Hebrew letters that can be adorned with "tagin" or "little crowns": SHIN (ש), AYIN (ע), TET (ט), NUN (נ), ZAYIN (ז), GIMEL (ג), and TSADIK (צ). All of these "little crowns" Hebrew letters each contain the letter ZAYIN (ז). [16] Not surprisingly, ZAYIN (ז) also represents the crowned man.

---

[16] *The Book of Letters: A Mystical Alef-bait* by Lawrence Kushner. ז. p. 37

Thoughts

Another aspect of the Word of God's sword is the Seven Spirits of God. The flaming sword going every which way to guard the way to the Tree of Life (Gen. 3:24) is linked to the seven torches before God's Throne: *"Seven lamps of fire were burning before the throne, which are the Seven Spirits of God"* (Revelation 4:5). The Golden Temple Menorah consisted of the central stem denoting the *Spirit of God* with six arms radiating outward, three on each side. [17] According to Scripture, the seven lights of the Temple Menorah map to the Seven Spirits of God. *"There shall come forth a Rod from the stem of Jesse, And a Branch shall grow out of his roots. ² The Spirit of the Lord shall rest upon Him, The Spirit of wisdom and understanding, The Spirit of counsel and might, The Spirit of knowledge and of the fear of the Lord"* (Isaiah 11:1-2).

Messiah Yeshua is pure white light while the Seven Spirits of God are the rainbow colors that make up that spotless white light. These seven make up the Nature of Christ:

[1] Red—Spirit of the Lord

[2] Orange—Spirit of Wisdom

[3] Yellow—Spirit of Understanding

[4] Green—Spirit of Counsel

[5] Light Blue—Spirit of Might/Power/Strength

[6] Indigo—Spirit of Knowledge/Revelation

[7] Purple—Spirit of the Fear of the Lord

The Lord has shown me that the Seven Spirits of God are unique to mankind. When God formed man of the dust into a clay vessel of the ground, He breathed into his nostrils the "breath of life." *"And the Lord God formed man of the dust of the ground, and breathed into his nostrils the breath of life; and man became a living being"* (Genesis 2:7). The first mention of God's Name YHVH (יהוה) is when God breathed *nishmat chayim* into man and he became a living soul made in God's own image through the impartation of the Seven Spirits of God.

YHVH (יהוה) is a unique word, which means God is present (Exo. 3:14) and God is lovingkindness and mercy (Exo. 34:6-7). Each of the four letters of YHVH are vowel sounds. They suggest God's Spirit is as close as our breath—our very life. *"The Spirit of God has made me, And the breath of the Almighty gives me life"* (Job 33:4). Thus, the Seven Spirits of God have been woven throughout a person's body, soul, and spirit, making each individual a temple of the Holy Spirit. Much more revelation about the Seven Spirits of God resides in the *Quantum 22™: The Hebrew Living™ Letters* book.

---

[17] *The Wisdom of the Hebrew Alphabet* by Rabbi Michael L. Munk, p. 106

Thoughts

The Way Of Wisdom

1. How can you do the sword dance with the double-edged sword? Hint: Study Heb. 4.

_____

_____

_____

2. What are some ways that you can engage the Seven Spirits of God? Hint: Study Scriptural references for each; and then, apply what you learn. For example, you can study references to the word "wisdom" for the Spirit of Wisdom (Isa. 11:2).

"Spirit of the Lord" _____

_____

_____

"Spirit of Wisdom" _____

_____

_____

"Spirit of Understanding" _____

_____

_____

"Spirit of Counsel" _____

_____

_____

"Spirit of Might" _____

_____

_____

"Spirit of Knowledge" _____

_____

_____

"Spirit of the Fear of the Lord" _____

_____

_____

3. What does it mean to you that the Word of God is a discerner of the thoughts and intents of the heart? Check out Hebrews 4:12 and Psalms 19:14.

_____

_____

_____

4. What are some specifics surrounding Messiah Yeshua being called The Word of God in Revelation 19:13? Yeshua sits on a white horse (Rev. 19:11).

_____

_____

He is clothed with a robe dipped in blood (Rev. 19:13).

_____

_____

Armies clothed in fine white linen follow Him on white horses (Rev. 19:14).

_____

_____

Out of ALEF-TAV's mouth comes a sharp sword (Rev. 19:15).

_____

_____

Written on His thigh is His title King of Kings and Lord of Lords (Rev. 19:16).

_____

_____

5. What comes to mind when you think about the words of the LORD being pure, like silver refined seven times (Psalms 12:6)?

_____

_____

_____

6. Research various references to the phrase "Word of God". For instance:

*"Every **word of God** is pure; He is a shield to those who put their trust in Him" (Prov. 30:5).*

_____

_____

_____

*"Making the **word of God** of no effect through your tradition which you have handed down" (Mark 7:13).*

_____

_____

_____

*"But Jesus answered him, saying, 'It is written, "Man shall not live by bread alone, but by every **word of God**" ' " (Luke 4:4).*

_____

_____

_____

*"So it was, as the multitude pressed about Him to hear the **word of God**" (Luke 5:1).*

_____

_____

_____

*"So then faith comes by hearing, and hearing by the **word of God**" (Rom. 10:17).*

_____

_____

_____

*"For we are not, as so many, peddling the **word of God**; but as of sincerity, but as from God, we speak in the sight of God in Christ" (2 Cor. 2:17).*

_____

_____

_____

*"By faith we understand that the worlds were framed by the **word of God**, so that the things which are seen were not made of things which are visible" (Heb. 11:3).*

_____

_____

_____

ZAYIN (ז)

Which ALEF-TAV (את) element of the Word of God,
included in the wisdom of ZAYIN (ז), is the sharpest truth for you?

PRACTICE WRITING ZAYIN

● Pronounced *ZAH-yeen* ●

Start to the left at the top. Make a short downward-sloping line toward your right. Next, bring your pen just right of center below the top line you just drew so you can draw a line straight down to the bottom line.

is the letter of a sword and a seed
ZERA (זֶרַע). The sword of the
Spirit, which is the Word of God,
has seven flaming flows . . . the
Spirit of the Lord, the Spirit of
Wisdom, the Spirit of
Understanding, the Spirit of
Counsel, the Spirit of Might, the
Spirit of Knowledge, and the
Spirit of the Fear of the Lord.
These Seven Spirits of God
contain the incorruptible seed
of the Word of God.

CHET/HET (ח)

CHET (ח) is the eighth *Hebrew Living™ Letter* of the Alef-Bet whose pronunciation rhymes with "met." It has the sound of "ch" as in Bach. CHET (ח) has the numerical value of 8, which means that the Hebrews use it for the number 8.

The ancient pictograph for CHET (ח) agrees with the meaning of its name. In ancient Hebrew CHET means a fence or an inner room. Its pictograph of fence symbolizes separating, cutting off, or protecting. [18]

CHET (ח) IN ALEF-TAV (את)

You and I can personally choose to engage the essence of Messiah Yeshua—the Word of God—contained within the Hebrew letter CHET (ח). Since CHET (ח) in Ancient Hebrew means a fence or an inner room, one of the most direct ALEF-TAV (את) redemptions for this Hebrew letter has to do with defense, because the word "fence" essentially communicates defense.

There is no shortage of Scriptures that refer to the Lord as the defense of His people: *"God is my defense"* (Psalms 59:9,16) and *"The Lord is my defense; and my God is the rock of my refuge"* (Psalms 94:22) and *"The Lord is our defense; and the Holy One of Israel is our king"* (Psalms 89:18). Clearly, the LORD our God is de-fence that surrounds His people.

A fence is a barrier of protection that encloses an area. It marks a boundary and controls access. *"'For I,' says the Lord, 'will be a wall of fire all around her, and I will be the glory in her midst'"* (Zechariah 2:5).

ALEF-TAV (את)'s CHET (ח) connection to an inner room is the holiest innermost chamber of His Dwelling Place:

> *"²³ For the <u>inner sanctuary</u> he made a pair of cherubim out of olive wood, each ten cubits high. ²⁴ One wing of the first cherub was five cubits long, and the other wing five cubits—ten cubits from wing tip to wing tip. ²⁵ The second cherub also measured ten cubits, for the two cherubim were identical in size and shape. ²⁶ The height of each cherub was ten cubits. ²⁷ He placed the cherubim inside the <u>innermost room of the temple</u>, with their wings spread out. The wing of one cherub touched one wall, while the wing of the other touched the other wall, and their wings touched each other in the middle of the room. ²⁸ He overlaid the cherubim with gold. ²⁹ On the walls all around the temple, in both the inner and outer rooms, he carved cherubim, palm trees and open flowers. ³⁰ He also covered the floors of both the inner and outer rooms of the temple with gold"* (2 Kings 6:23-30).

---

[18] *Hebrew Word Pictures* by Frank T. Seekins, Chet, p. 40

Besides the Almighty's connection to a fence or inner room, another substantial ALEF-TAV (את) redemption for the Hebrew letter CHET (ח) has to do with life itself . . . eternal life.

I pay particular attention to any statement preceded with "I am." due to various Scriptures, like: *"To Him who loved us and washed us from our sins in His own blood, ⁶ and has made us kings and priests to His God and Father, to Him be glory and dominion forever and ever. Amen. ⁷ Behold, He is coming with clouds, and every eye will see Him, even they who pierced Him. And all the tribes of the earth will mourn because of Him. Even so, Amen ⁸ 'I am the Alpha [ALEF] and the Omega [TAV], the Beginning and the End,' says the Lord, 'who is and who was and who is to come, the Almighty' " (Revelation 1:5b-8* ₐddᵢₜᵢₒₙₛ ₘᵢₙₑ*).*

Whenever you see the phrase "I am" think of ALEF-TAV (את)—Almighty God. In particular, let's examine Messiah Yeshua in regard to the terms "I am" and "life." *"Jesus said to him, 'I am the way, the truth, and the life. No one comes to the Father except through Me' " (John 14:6).*

Yeshua plainly declares "I am the resurrection" along with His proclamation "I am the life" while He was raising Lazarus from the dead.

> *" ²⁵ Jesus said to her, 'I am the resurrection and the life. He who believes in Me, though he may die, he shall live. ²⁶ And whoever lives and believes in Me shall never die. Do you believe this?' ²⁷ She said to Him, 'Yes, Lord, I believe that You are the Christ, the Son of God, who is to come into the world' " (John 11:25-27).*

The life we experience comes from ALEF-TAV (את):

> *" ¹ In the beginning was the Word, and the Word was with God, and the Word was God. ² He was in the beginning with God. ³ All things were made through Him, and without Him nothing was made that was made. ⁴ In Him was life, and the life was the light of men" (John 1:1-4).*

Eternal life is for those who believe in the death, burial, and resurrection of Messiah Yeshua:

> *" ¹⁴ And as Moses lifted up the serpent in the wilderness, even so must the Son of Man be lifted up, ¹⁵ that whoever believes in Him should not perish but have eternal life. ¹⁶ For God so loved the world that He gave His only begotten Son, that whoever believes in Him should not perish but have everlasting life" (John 3:14-16).*

According to the power of an endless life, ALEF-TAV (את) arose as a priest. Fundamentally, the righteous Order of Melchizedek is based on the eternal life of its High Priest Yeshua:

> *" ¹⁴ For it is evident that our Lord arose from Judah, of which tribe Moses spoke nothing concerning priesthood. ¹⁵ And it is yet far more evident if, in the likeness of Melchizedek, there arises another priest ¹⁶ who has come, not according to the law of a fleshly commandment, but according to the power of an endless life. ¹⁷ For He testifies: 'You are a priest forever according to the Order of Melchizedek' " (Hebrews 7:14-17).*

CHET is the Hebrew letter most known for its connection to life. [19] As we have seen, Scripture speaks of the breath of life through which God created man (Gen. 2:7). The breath of the Almighty gives mankind life (Job 33:4).

There is the Tree of Life in the midst of the garden east of Eden: *"And out of the ground the Lord God made every tree grow that is pleasant to the sight and good for food. The Tree of Life was also in the midst of the garden, and the Tree of the Knowledge of good and evil"* (Genesis 2:9). Those who eat of the Tree of Life live forever: *"Then the Lord God said, 'Behold, the man has become like one of Us, to know good and evil. And now, lest he put out his hand and take also of the Tree of Life, and eat, and live forever'"* (Genesis 3:22). However, since the Fall of Adam and Eve, Cherubim and a flaming sword guard the way to the Tree of Life: *"Then the Lord God said, 'So He drove out the man; and He placed cherubim at the east of the garden of Eden, and a flaming sword which turned every way, to guard the way to the Tree of Life'"* (Genesis 3:24).

There is a pure river of the Water of Life proceeding from The Throne:

> ***"And he showed me a pure river of Water of Life, clear as crystal, proceeding from the throne of God and of the Lamb"*** (Revelation 22:1). On either side of the river is the Tree of Life: ***"In the middle of its street, and on either side of the river, was the Tree of Life, which bore twelve fruits, each tree yielding its fruit every month. The leaves of the tree were for the healing of the nations"*** (Revelation 22:2).

ALEF-TAV (את) gives of the fountain of the "Water of Life" freely:

> ***"And He said to me, 'It is done! I am the Alpha [ALEF] and the Omega [TAV], the Beginning and the End. I will give of the fountain of the water of life freely to him who thirsts'"*** (Revelation 21:6 Additions mine).

The LORD established the earth upon the waters:

> ***"The earth is the Lord's, and all its fullness, The world and those who dwell therein. For He has founded it upon the seas, And established it upon the waters"*** (Psalms 24:1-2).

No wonder the letter CHET (ח) is an acronym for "life" (חַיִּים). The human body is brought to life when the Seven Spirits of God-infused soul (נְשָׁמָה) enters a person's body. Please refer to the *Quantum 22™: The Hebrew Living™ Letters* book for more on this subject.

IN THE MIDST of God's Kingdom is the pure river of the water of life that comes from the throne with the Tree of Life on either side.

> ***"And he showed me a pure river of water of life, clear as crystal, proceeding from the throne of God and of the Lamb. In the middle of its street, and on either side of the river, was the Tree of Life, which bore twelve fruits, each tree yielding its fruit every month. The leaves of the tree were for the healing of the nations. And there shall be no more curse, but the throne of God and of the Lamb shall be in it, and His servants shall serve Him"*** (Revelation 22:1-3).

---

[19] *The Wisdom of the Hebrew Alphabet* by Rabbi Michael L. Munk, p. 114

IN THE MIDST of God's Kingdom is the River of Life with which the Messiah's Bride is cleansed by the washing of water with the word: He is good . . . He is good . . . He is good . . .

> *"That He might sanctify and cleanse it with the washing of water by the Word. That He might present it to Himself a glorious church, not having spot, or wrinkle, or any such thing; but that it should be holy and without blemish" (Ephesians 5:26-27 KJV).*

Taking communion is connected to eternal life:

> *"Then Jesus said to them, 'Most assuredly, I say to you, unless you eat the flesh of the Son of Man and drink His blood, you have no life in you. Whoever eats My flesh and drinks My blood has eternal life, and I will raise him up at the last day' " (John 6:53-54).* True knowledge of our Heavenly Father and the Son is eternal life: *"And this is eternal life, that they may know You, the only true God, and Jesus Christ whom You have sent" (John 17:3).*

In ALEF-TAV (את) is the life and light of men: *"³ All things were made through Him, and without Him nothing was made that was made. ⁴ In Him was life, and the life was the light of men" (John 1:3-4).* When you follow Yeshua, you have the Light of Life: *"Then Jesus spoke to them again, saying, 'I am the light of the world. He who follows Me shall not walk in darkness, but have the light of life' " (John 8:12).* Messiah Yeshua has life in Himself, just like Our Heavenly Father: *"For as the Father has life in Himself, so He has granted the Son to have life in Himself" (John 5:26).*

ALEF-TAV (את) is the Bread of Life:

> *" 'For the bread of God is He who comes down from heaven and gives life to the world.' Then they said to Him, 'Lord, give us this bread always.' And Jesus said to them, 'I am the bread of life. He who comes to Me shall never hunger, and he who believes in Me shall never thirst' " (John 6:33-35).*

There is life in the Messiah's Name:

> *"And truly Jesus did many other signs in the presence of His disciples, which are not written in this book; ³¹ but these are written that you may believe that Jesus is the Christ, the Son of God, and that believing you may have life in His name" (John 20:30-31).*

Thoughts

The Way Of Wisdom

1. How has God been your defense? Record a specific example for gratefulness' sake.

_____

_____

_____

2. What picture of "life" resonates most with you and why?

Breath of **Life** (Gen. 2:7). _____

_____

_____

Tree of **Life** (Gen. 2:9, 3:22). _____

_____

_____

Water of **Life** (Rev. 22:1). _____

_____

_____

Priesthood based on the power of endless **life** (Heb. 7:15-17). _____

_____

_____

3. Why do you think ALEF-TAV (את) gives the water of life freely?

_____

_____

_____

_____

_____

4. More thoroughly investigate the following "I am" statements of Messiah Yeshua.

"**I am** the bread of life" (John 6:35,41,48). _____

_____

_____

"**I am** the light of the world" (John 8:12, 9:5). _____
_____
_____

"**I am** the door" (John 10:7,9). _____
_____
_____

"**I am** the good shepherd" (John 10:11,14). _____
_____
_____

"**I am** the Son of God" (John 10:36). _____
_____
_____

"**I am** the resurrection and the life" (John 11:25). _____
_____
_____

"**I am** the Way and the Truth and the Life" (John 14:6). _____
_____
_____

"**I am** in the Father" (John 14:10-11,20). _____
_____
_____

"**I am** the vine" (John 15:5). _____
_____
_____

"**I am** not of the world" (John 17:16). _____
_____
_____

"**I am** a king" (John 18:37). _____

_____

_____

"**I am** ascending to My Father and your Father" (John 20:17). _____

_____

_____

5. Why do you think God put Cherubim with a flaming sword to guard/keep the way to the Tree of Life (Gen 3:24)?

_____

_____

_____

_____

_____

_____

6. What causes you to have the light of life? Refer to John 8:12.

_____

_____

_____

_____

_____

7. What comes to mind with the phrase "the power of endless life"? See. Hebrews 7.

_____

_____

_____

_____

_____

CHET (ח)

What ALEF-TAV (את) jewel of life, included in the wisdom of CHET (ח), is most powerful for you?

PRACTICE WRITING CHET

♦ CHET's pronunciation rhymes with "met." It has the sound of "ch" as in Bach ♦

Start to the left at the top and draw a straight line to the right with a bend downward. Continue to draw a vertical line to the bottom line. Then, come back to the beginning point and draw a line straight downward.

is an acronym for "life" —
CHAIM (חַיִּים). The human body
is brought to life when the Seven
Spirits of God infused soul
(נְשָׁמָה) enters a person's body.
Throughout our lives, we
physically exist mostly as water.
Behold, in the midst of the
Kingdom of God within you is
the pure river of the water of life
that comes from His Throne with
the Tree of Life on either side.

WISDOM ELEVEN

ט
TET

TET/TES (ט)

TET (ט) is the ninth *Hebrew Living™ Letter* of the Alef-Bet whose pronunciation rhymes with "mate." It has the sound of "t" as in tall. TET (ט) has the numerical value of 9, which means that the Hebrews use it for the number 9.

The ancient pictograph for TET (ט) agrees with the meaning of its name. In ancient Hebrew, TET means a snake or to surround, Its pictograph of something twisted around symbolizes surrounding or twisting. [20]

TET (ט) IN ALEF-TAV (את)

You and I can personally choose to engage the essence of Messiah Yeshua—the Word of God—contained within the Hebrew letter TET (ט).

One of the most direct ALEF-TAV (את) redemptions for this Hebrew letter has to do with Messiah Yeshua being lifted up on the Cross, just like the serpent in the wilderness:

> *"[13] No one has ascended to heaven but He who came down from heaven, that is, the Son of Man who is in heaven. [14] And as Moses lifted up the serpent in the wilderness, even so must the Son of Man be lifted up, [15] that whoever believes in Him should not perish but have eternal life" (John 3:13-15).*

The first occurrence of the word "snake" ("serpent") is in Genesis 3. This first mention illustrates the serpent as the tempter, the deceiver, and the instigator of sin.

> *"[1] Now the <u>serpent</u> was more cunning than any beast of the field which the Lord God had made. And he said to the woman, 'Has God indeed said, "You shall not eat of every tree of the garden"?' [2] And the woman said to the serpent, 'We may eat the fruit of the trees of the garden; [3] but of the fruit of the tree which is in the midst of the garden, God has said, "You shall not eat it, nor shall you touch it, lest you die." ' [4] Then the <u>serpent</u> said to the woman, 'You will not surely die. [5] For God knows that in the day you eat of it your eyes will be opened, and you will be like God, knowing good and evil' " (Genesis 3:1-4).*

---

[20] *Hebrew Word Pictures* by Frank T. Seekins, Tet, p. 44

" ¹³ And the Lord God said to the woman, 'What is this you have done?' The woman said, 'The serpent deceived me, and I ate.' ¹⁴ So the Lord God said to the serpent: 'Because you have done this, You are cursed more than all cattle, And more than every beast of the field; On your belly you shall go, And you shall eat dust all the days of your life. ¹⁵ And I will put enmity between you and the woman, And between your seed and her Seed; He shall bruise your head, And you shall bruise His heel' " (Genesis 3:13-15).

The serpent has been cursed by God himself to eat the dust of the earth. What is mankind's flesh made out of? *"And the Lord God formed man of the dust of the ground, and breathed into his nostrils the breath of life; and man became a living being" (Genesis 2:7).* Therefore, be encouraged when you face various trials; because *Ha Satan* (the whole satanic kingdom) has a purpose. The old serpent and his slithery entourage have a God-ordained purpose, which is to eat up, consume, and get rid of the dust of your earth—your fleshly, carnal nature.

According to the Midrash, TET (ט) alludes to mud (טיט), and is symbolic of physical matter, from which man's body was created. Man is in the Almighty's hand as clay is in the potter's hand (Jeremiah 18:6). [21]

Back to *"as Moses lifted up the serpent in the wilderness, even so must the Son of Man be lifted up" (John 3:14)*. Before Yeshua was lifted up on the Cross to die once-for-all, Moses led a stiff-necked people in the Wilderness for forty years. When the people complained against Moses, fiery serpents swarmed them, causing many to die from their poison. The people begged Moses to forgive them and remove this curse from their camp. They sincerely repented due to the severe consequences. In response to their genuine repentance, God instructed Moses to do something quite bizarre:

" ⁸ Then the Lord said to Moses, 'Make a fiery serpent, and set it on a pole; and it shall be that everyone who is bitten, when he looks at it, shall live.' ⁹ So Moses made a bronze serpent, and put it on a pole; and so it was, if a serpent had bitten anyone, when he looked at the bronze serpent, he lived" (Numbers 21:8-9).

God required them to gaze upon a brazen image of the very image that was killing them. The fiery brazen serpent was hinting at the antidote of Brazen Altar to the serpent itself. Imagine being bitten and the only way to escape death is to look up at the serpent on a pole. God knew that the fiery serpent would be a repulsive sight.

Employing a brazen serpent to cure serpent bites may seem ironic, but it's the nature of homeopathic medical science. *Similia similibys curentur* means "let likes be treated with likes." This is when the Cross of Christ comes in.

" ³² 'And I, if I am lifted up from the earth, will draw all peoples to Myself.' ³³ This He said, signifying by what death He would die" (John 12:32-33).

---

[21] *The Wisdom of the Hebrew Alphabet* by Rabbi Michael L. Munk, p. 119

Thoughts

"Then Jesus said to them, 'When you lift up the Son of Man, then you will know that I am He, and that I do nothing of Myself; but as My Father taught Me, I speak these things' " *(John 8:28).*

It is significant to note that the brazen serpent, which God directed Moses to lift up in the desert later became an idol because they exalted a thing rather than the Source—ALEF-TAV (את). When King Hezekiah cleansed the land of Israel, *"He removed the high places and broke the sacred pillars, cut down the wooden image and broke in pieces the bronze serpent that Moses had made; for until those days the children of Israel burned incense to it, and called it Nehushtan"* *(2 Kings 18:4).* *"Nehushtan"* literally means a bronze thing and it's similar to the Hebrew word *nahash* (נחש), which means serpent.

TET (ט) is the least common letter in the Hebrew Bible. There are only 100 words in the Hebrew Bible starting with the Hebrew letter TET. Of these 15 are proper names and 85 are regular words.

The first TET (ט) that appears in the Bible is in the Hebrew word—*"tov"* (טוב)—which means "good." *"And God saw the light, that it was good, and God divided the light from the darkness"* *(Genesis 1:4).* This speaks of the letter (ט) representing goodness. Significantly, *tov* is used seven times in the first chapter of Genesis.

God is the essence of all good—*tov:*

"Praise the Lord of hosts, For the Lord is good, For His mercy endures forever '—And of those who will bring the sacrifice of praise into the house of the Lord. For I will cause the captives of the land to return as at the first,' says the Lord" *(Jeremiah 33:11).*

All He created is very good: *"Then God saw everything that He had made, and indeed it was very good. So the evening and the morning were the sixth day"* *(Genesis 1:31).* The world that God created during the six days of Creation is very good. Notice how God evaluated His labor on each day of Creation. He pronounced a righteous judgment over it: *"it was good"* *(Genesis 1:4,10,12,18,21,25).*

When a person follows the guidelines set by the Creator, the world remains good. And even when man pollutes the world physically or spiritually, God grants him the gift of repentance. Mankind longs for a good life, good health, good business, and a good year; but what is good? Success is often ephemeral (lasts a short time) and prosperity corrupting, while setbacks and adversity often set the stage for advancement and triumph. Only God knows what is truly, objectively good for man.[22]

---

[22] *The Wisdom of the Hebrew Alphabet* by Rabbi Michael L. Munk, p. 119

Thoughts

The Way Of Wisdom

1. How can you lift up the Son of Man in your own life? Hint: John 3:14, John 8:28.

_____

_____

_____

2. When we combine that the serpent has been cursed to eat up the dust of the earth with the fact that our flesh is made out of the dust of the earth, we understand that the serpent of old—the Devil—has a purpose. His purpose is to consume our fleshly, carnal nature. How can this awareness make your trials in life easier to go through?

_____

_____

_____

_____

3. Dig deeper into the seven references of what God says is "good" in Genesis 1:

Genesis 1:4. _____

_____

_____

Genesis 1:10. _____

_____

_____

Genesis 1:12. _____

_____

_____

Genesis 1:18. _____

_____

_____

Genesis 1:21. _____

_____

_____

Genesis 1:25. _____

_____

_____

Genesis 1:31. _____

_____

_____

4. Research and apply various references to the crux of the "cross" of Christ from the four gospels of Matthew, Mark, Luke, and John.

*"Likewise the chief priests also, mocking with the scribes and elders, said, [42] 'He saved others; Himself He cannot save. If He is the King of Israel, let Him now come down from the **cross**, and we will believe Him'"* (Matthew 27:41-42).

_____

_____

_____

_____

_____

*"Then Jesus said to His disciples, 'If anyone desires to come after Me, let him deny himself, and take up his **cross**, and follow Me'"* (Matthew 16:24).

_____

_____

_____

_____

*"When He had called the people to Himself, with His disciples also, He said to them, 'Whoever desires to come after Me, let him deny himself, and take up his **cross**, and follow Me'"* (Mark 8:34).

_____

_____

_____

_____

_____

*"Then He said to them all, 'If anyone desires to come after Me, let him deny himself, and take up his **cross** daily, and follow Me'" (Luke 9:23).*

_____

_____

_____

_____

*"And He, bearing His **cross**, went out to a place called the Place of a Skull, which is called in Hebrew, Golgotha, ¹⁸ where they crucified Him, and two others with Him, one on either side, and Jesus in the center. ¹⁹ Now Pilate wrote a title and put it on the **cross**. And the writing was: JESUS OF NAZARETH, THE KING OF THE JEWS" (John 19:17-19).*

_____

_____

_____

_____

*"Therefore, because it was the Preparation Day, that the bodies should not remain on the **cross** on the Sabbath (for that Sabbath was a high day), the Jews asked Pilate that their legs might be broken, and that they might be taken away. ³² Then the soldiers came and broke the legs of the first and of the other who was crucified with Him. ³³ But when they came to Jesus and saw that He was already dead, they did not break His legs. ³⁴ But one of the soldiers pierced His side with a spear, and immediately blood and water came out. ³⁵ And he who has seen has testified, and his testimony is true; and he knows that he is telling the truth, so that you may believe. ³⁶ For these things were done that the Scripture should be fulfilled, 'Not one of His bones shall be broken.' ³⁷ And again another Scripture says, 'They shall look on Him whom they pierced'" (John 19:31-37).*

_____

_____

_____

_____

5. Don't forget to add the "crucified" references to your "cross" walk and talk. There are many Scriptures that have "crucified" in their verses. Here is a sampling to get you started.

The Son of Man will be **crucified** (Matt. 26:2). _____

_____

_____

_____

"Let Him be **crucified**" (Matt. 27:22-23). _____

_____

_____

Pilate had Jesus scourged and delivered Him to be **crucified** (Matt. 27:26). _____

_____

_____

They mocked Yeshua and led Him away to be **crucified** (Matt. 27:31). _____

_____

_____

_____

They **crucified** Yeshua and cast lots for His garments (Matt. 27:35). _____

_____

_____

_____

I know you seek Yeshua who was **crucified** (Matt. 28:5). _____

_____

_____

_____

Our old man was **crucified** with Christ (Rom. 6:6). _____

_____

_____

_____

I have been **crucified** in union with Christ; it is no longer I who live, but Christ lives in me; and the life which I now live in the flesh I live by the faith of the Son of God who loved me and gave Himself for me (Gal. 2:20).

_____

_____

_____

TET (ט)

What ALEF-TAV (את) wisdom gem about TET (ט) is highlighted in your spirit?

PRACTICE WRITING TET

♦ TET's pronunciation rhymes with "mate." It makes the sound of "t" as in tall ♦
Start at the top left and draw a swooping curve towards the right.

ט

is good—TOV (טוב). Not only does טוב mean to be good, but it also signifies to be pleasing, to be beneficial, to be delightful, and to be favorable. The sweet psalmist of Israel—King David—tells us that we can taste and see that the Lord is good. The earth is full of His goodness. The goodness of God endures forever. The LORD delights in the steps of every good person, and we are satisfied with the goodness of His house, which the LORD surrounds and makes secure.

WISDOM TWELVE

ﬞ

YUD

YUD/YOD/YOOD (י)

YUD (י) is the tenth *Hebrew Living™ Letter* of the Alef-Bet. Its pronunciation is *yood*, which rhymes with "mode." YUD (י) has the numerical value of 10, which means that the Hebrews use it for the number 10.

The ancient pictograph for YUD (י) agrees with the meaning of its name. In ancient Hebrew YUD means a hand, which symbolizes work or a deed done. [23]

YUD (י) IN ALEF-TAV (את)

You and I can personally choose to engage the essence of Messiah Yeshua—the Word of God—contained within the Hebrew letter YUD (י). The most direct ALEF-TAV (את) redemption for this Hebrew letter has to do with Messiah Yeshua being the "hand of the Lord."

> *"The king's heart is in the <u>hand of the Lord</u>, like the rivers of water; He turns it wherever He wishes. Every way of a man is right in his own eyes, but the Lord weighs the hearts" (Prov. 21:1-2).*

Take note that when the "hand of the Lord" is understood by His servants, His enemies know His indignation.

> *" ¹⁴ When you see this, your heart shall rejoice, And your bones shall flourish like grass; The <u>hand of the Lord</u> shall be known to His servants, And His indignation to His enemies. ¹⁵ For behold, the Lord will come with fire And with His chariots, like a whirlwind, To render His anger with fury, And His rebuke with flames of fire. ¹⁶ For by fire and by His sword The Lord will judge all flesh; And the slain of the Lord shall be many" (Isaiah 66:14-16).*

The "hand of the Lord" is also connected to chariots, fire, and a whirlwind in the Book of Ezekiel. Notice how the Word of the Lord is associated with the hand of the Lord in the following passage.

---

[23] *Hebrew Word Pictures* by Frank T. Seekins, Yood, p. 48

"³ The word of the Lord came expressly to Ezekiel the priest, the son of Buzi, in the land of the Chaldeans by the River Chebar; and the <u>hand of the Lord</u> was upon him there. ⁴ Then I looked, and behold, a whirlwind was coming out of the north, a great cloud with raging fire engulfing itself; and brightness was all around it and radiating out of its midst like the color of amber, out of the midst of the fire. ⁵ Also from within it came the likeness of four living creatures. And this was their appearance: they had the likeness of a man" (Ezekiel 1:3-5).*

Both the Egyptians and the Israelites understood that the "hand of the Lord" is mighty. With His holy touch, they experienced the reverential fear of the Lord. *"¹ Then the Lord said to Moses, 'Go in to Pharaoh and tell him, "Thus says the Lord God of the Hebrews: 'Let My people go, that they may serve Me. ² For if you refuse to let them go, and still hold them, ³ behold, the <u>hand of the Lord</u> will be on your cattle in the field, on the horses, on the donkeys, on the camels, on the oxen, and on the sheep—a very severe pestilence. ⁴ And the Lord will make a difference between the livestock of Israel and the livestock of Egypt. So nothing shall die of all that belongs to the children of Israel.'"'"* (Exodus 9:1-4). The hand of the Lord's livestock plague change the dynamics because up until this plague, the Egyptian magicians had been able to duplicate them (at least they came close enough to dupe Pharaoh).

Just like the Red Sea crossing, the Israelites crossed over the Jordan River on dry ground so that all the peoples of the earth would know that the "hand of the Lord" is mighty:

"²¹ Then he spoke to the children of Israel, saying: 'When your children ask their fathers in time to come, saying, "What are these stones?" ²² then you shall let your children know, saying, "Israel crossed over this Jordan on dry land"; ²³ for the Lord your God dried up the waters of the Jordan before you until you had crossed over, as the Lord your God did to the Red Sea, which He dried up before us until we had crossed over, ²⁴ that all the peoples of the earth may know the <u>hand of the Lord</u>, that it is mighty, that you may fear the Lord your God forever'" (Joshua 4:21-24).

YUD (׳) is 10. Just as there were ten plagues to force Pharaoh to release God's people so they could worship Him, the Hebrews record ten miracles at the Red Sea:

[1] The sea split;

[2] the water formed a tent over their heads;

[3] the land became firm (not muddy);

[4] the land turned muddy when Egyptians tried to cross;

[5] the sea split into 12 strips so each tribe could travel separately;

[6] the water froze and became as hard as a rock;

[7] the water which became rock was actually many rocks beautifully arranged;

[8] the water remained clear so the tribes could see each other;

[9] water that was fit for drinking leaked from all sides;

[10] after they finished drinking the water, the water immediately froze again. [24]

---

[24]*Mishnah 5:5,* Ramban

The right hand of the Lord is exalted and does valiantly. It is fearless, noble, bold, and indomitable.

" [15] The voice of rejoicing and salvation is in the tents of the righteous; The <u>right hand of the Lord</u> does valiantly. [16] The <u>right hand of the Lord</u> is exalted; The <u>right hand of the Lord</u> does valiantly. [17] I shall not die, but live, And declare the works of the Lord. [18] The Lord has chastened me severely, But He has not given me over to death. [19] Open to me the gates of righteousness; I will go through them, And I will praise the Lord. [20] This is the gate of the Lord, Through which the righteous shall enter" (Psalms 118:15-20).

YUD (י) is the smallest letter in the Hebrew Alef-Bet. It is barely larger than a dot and suspended in mid-air. Some say the shape of YUD resembles an apostrophe. YUD (י) is said to be the atom of the consonants, and the form by which all the other Hebrew letters begin and end.

To the Hebrew, "the first dot with which the scribes first start writing a letter, or the last dot that gives a letter its final form—is a yod." [25] Since YUD (י) is used to form all other letters, it indicates God's omnipresence. Additionally, since Yeshua upholds all things by the word of His power and YUD is part of every letter of the Hebrew Alphabet, YUD (י) is considered to be the spark of the Spirit in everything. In other words, YUD is considered to be the starting point of the Presence of God in all things (Hebrews 1:3).

"For with [His Name] YAH, HASHEM is the Rock of the Universe" (Isaiah 26:4). Through the study of Scripture and its nuances, many Hebrew Sages believe that God created the universe with the Hebrew letters YUD (י) and HEI (ה)—YAH (יָה). The name YAH is the shortened form of YHVH (יהוה). Not only is YUD the first Hebrew letter of YAH and YHVH, but it also begins the name of the Savior of the world—Yeshua (ישוע).

Additionally, YUD (י) is the first letter for the four names given to the Hebrews in Scripture: Ya'akov (יַעֲקֹב)—Jacob, Yisrael (יִשְׂרָאֵל)—Israel, Yehudi (יְהוּדִי)—Jews, and Yeshurun (יְשֻׁרוּן)—Jeshurun. [26] Note: There is no letter "j" in the Hebrew language.

Being the smallest of all letters, YUD (י) is a picture of humility. Take for example, when Jacob *(Ya'akov)* was renamed to Israel *(Yisrael)*, all that remained of his former name was the Hebrew letter YUD (י).

John the Baptist prepared the way of the Lord and so must we. John declared: *"He must increase, but I must decrease" (John 3:30).* This concept is also pictured in the Apostle Paul's name change. Paul means "little," which is the direct opposite of his previous name. The name Saul means "significant one" or "sought after." Decreasing or being made little is a transformation key for this Kingdom Day. We must decrease, so He can increase; however, we must also go the extra YUD (י) step. We must take on an extra YUD (י) as a mark of humility as Moses did. As the smallest Hebrew letter, YUD (י) is a picture of humility. There is an extra YUD (י) as a mark of humility in the text that says that Moses was the most humble man upon the face of the earth: *"(Now the man Moses was very humble, more than all men who were on the face of the earth.)" (Numbers 12:3).*

What is this extra YUD (י) mark of humility? Look to the Pattern Son: *" [5] Have this attitude in yourselves which was also in Christ Jesus, [6] who, as He already existed in the form of God, did not consider equality with God something to be grasped, [7] but emptied Himself by taking the form of a bond-servant and being born in the likeness of men. [8] And being found in appearance as a man, He humbled Himself by becoming obedient to the point of death: death on a cross" (Philippians 2:5-8* NASB *).* We must decrease, so He can increase AND we must disappear (die to ourselves), so He can appear in His glory.

---

[25] Likutei Maharan
[26] *The Wisdom of the Hebrew Alphabet* by Rabbi Michael L. Munk, p. 119

The Way Of Wisdom

1. How have you seen the "hand of the Lord" at work in your own life or others?

_____

_____

_____

2. Contemplate that YUD (׳) is used to form all other letters and is part of every letter of the Hebrew Alphabet. What are your thoughts?

_____

_____

_____

3. Why do you think that an extra YUD (׳) is a mark of humility? Refer to Numbers 12:3.

_____

_____

_____

4. How many plagues were before the livestock plague when the Lord made a distinction between the livestock of Israel and the livestock of Egypt (Exodus 19:1-4)? How did the hand of the Lord's plague change the dynamics?

_____

_____

_____

5. What were the ten plagues of Egypt? Research how they were connected to the Egyptian gods.

[1] Waters become blood (Exodus 7:14-25). _____

_____

_____

[2] Frogs (Exodus 8:1-15). _____
_____
_____

[3] Lice (Exodus 8:16-19). _____
_____
_____

[4] Flies (Exodus 8:20-32). _____
_____
_____

[5] Livestock (Exodus 9:1-7). _____
_____
_____

[6] Boils (Exodus 9:8-12). _____
_____
_____

[7] Hail (Exodus 9:13-35). _____
_____
_____

[8] Locust (Exodus 10:1-20). _____
_____
_____

[9] Darkness (Exodus 10:21-29). _____
_____
_____

[10] Death of the Firstborn (Exodus 12:29-30). _____
_____
_____

6. Contemplate the ten miracles at the Red Sea. Which ones draw your attention the most and why?

_____

_____

_____

_____

7. Research what the Bible says about YUD (׳) symbolizing work or a deed done.

*"Sing praises to the LORD, who dwells in Zion! Declare His **deeds** among the people" (Psa. 9:11).*

_____

_____

_____

_____

*"I will also meditate on all Your **work**, And talk of Your **deeds**" (Psa. 77:12).*

_____

_____

_____

_____

*"Thus they provoked Him to anger with their **deeds**, And the plague broke out among them" (Psa. 106:29).*

_____

_____

_____

_____

*"Thus they were defiled by their own **works**, And played the harlot by their own **deeds**" (Psa. 106:39).*

_____

_____

_____

_____

*"Even a child is known by his **deeds**, Whether what he does is pure and right"* (Prov. 20:11).

_____

_____

_____

_____

*"Take heed that you do not do your charitable **deeds** before men, to be seen by them. Otherwise you have no reward from your Father in heaven"* (Matt. 6:1).

_____

_____

_____

_____

*"And this is the condemnation, that the light has come into the world, and men loved darkness rather than light, because their **deeds** were evil. 20 For everyone practicing evil hates the light and does not come to the light, lest his **deeds** should be exposed. 21 But he who does the truth comes to the light, that his **deeds** may be clearly seen, that they have been done in God"* (John 3:19-21).

_____

_____

_____

_____

*"And whatever you do in word or **deed**, do all in the name of the Lord Jesus, giving thanks to God the Father through Him"* (Col. 3:17).

_____

_____

_____

_____

_____

_____

YUD (י)

What fundamental feature of ALEF-TAV (את)'s Hebrew letter YUD (י) is a high point for you?

PRACTICE WRITING YUD

◆ YUD is pronounced *yood*, which rhymes with "mode" ◆
Start at the top left and draw an apostrophe down to the center line.

י

is like a dove—YONA (יוֹנָה)—
which descends from heaven to
gently alight and remain on His
pleasing ones, just like the Pattern
Son who is the Son of God.
Those who adore Him have the
singleness of vision of dove eyes
with an olive branch in their
mouth, proclaiming the good
tidings of peace that surpasses
all understanding.

KAF/KAPH (כ)

KAF (כ) is the eleventh *Hebrew Living™ Letter* of the Alef-Bet. It is pronounced *kaf,* which has the sound of "k" as in kite or king when the letter has a dagesh (dot in the center). KAF (כ) has an ordinal value of 11 and a numerical value of 20, which means that the Hebrews can use it for either the number 11 or 20.

The ancient pictograph for KAF (כ) agrees with the meaning of its name. In ancient Hebrew KAF means a palm of a hand or a wing. The pictograph of an open hand symbolizes to allow, to cover, to open, or to be enthroned. [27]

KAF (כ) IN ALEF-TAV (את)

You and I can personally choose to engage the essence of Messiah Yeshua—the Word of God—contained within the Hebrew letter KAF (כ). The ALEF-TAV (את) redemption for this Hebrew letter has to do with the protective palm of Messiah Yeshua's hand.

> " [13] *Sing, O heavens! Be joyful, O earth! And break out in singing, O mountains! For the Lord has comforted His people, And will have mercy on His afflicted.* [14] *But Zion said, 'The Lord has forsaken me, And my Lord has forgotten me.'* [15] *'Can a woman forget her nursing child, And not have compassion on the son of her womb? Surely they may forget, Yet I will not forget you.* [16] *See, I have inscribed you on the <u>palms of My hands</u>; Your walls are continually before Me' "* (Isaiah 49:13-16).

Not only does KAF (כ) symbolizes God's protective palm, but God is all-knowing—omniscient:

> *"O Lord, You have searched me and known me.* [2] *You know my sitting down and my rising up; You understand my thought afar off.* [3] *You comprehend my path and my lying down, and are acquainted with all my ways.* [4] *For there is not a word on my tongue, But behold, O Lord, You know it altogether.* [5] *You have hedged me behind and before, And laid <u>Your hand</u> [KAF] upon me.* [6] *Such knowledge is too wonderful for me; It is high, I cannot attain it"* (Psalms 139:1-6 _{Additions mine}).

---

[27] *Hebrew Word Pictures* by Frank T. Seekins, Kaf, p. 52

The other ALEF-TAV (את) redemption for KAF (כ) is the Messiah's wings.

> " *9 For the Lord's portion is His people; Jacob is the place of His inheritance. 10 He found him in a desert land And in the wasteland, a howling wilderness; He encircled him, He instructed him, He kept him as the apple of His eye. 11 As an eagle stirs up its nest, Hovers over its young, Spreading out its <u>wings</u>, taking them up, Carrying them on its <u>wings</u>, 12 So the Lord alone led him, And there was no foreign god with him" (Deuteronomy 32:9-12).*

God instructs Moses to tell the children of Israel of His wings in Exodus 19.

> " *3 And Moses went up to God, and the Lord called to him from the mountain, saying, 'Thus you shall say to the house of Jacob, and tell the children of Israel: 4 You have seen what I did to the Egyptians, and how I bore you on eagles' <u>wings</u> and brought you to Myself. 5 Now therefore, if you will indeed obey My voice and keep My covenant, then you shall be a special treasure to Me above all people; for all the earth is Mine. 6 And you shall be to Me a kingdom of priests and a holy nation. These are the words which you shall speak to the children of Israel.' 7 So Moses came and called for the elders of the people, and laid before them all these words which the Lord commanded him 8 Then all the people answered together and said, 'All that the Lord has spoken we will do' " (Exodus 19:3-8).*

The wonderful kinsmen-redeemer—Boaz—spoke this incredible blessing over his future wife Ruth.

> *"The Lord repay your work, and a full reward be given you by the Lord God of Israel, under whose <u>wings</u> you have come for refuge" (Ruth 2:12).*

Boaz and Ruth's great-grandson David prayed:

> *"6 I have called upon You, for You will hear me, O God; Incline Your ear to me, and hear my speech. 7 Show Your marvelous lovingkindness by Your right hand, O You who save those who trust in You from those who rise up against them. 8 Keep me as the apple of Your eye; Hide me under the shadow of Your <u>wings</u>, 9 From the wicked who oppress me, From my deadly enemies who surround me" (Psalms 17:6-9).*

Thoughts

The Word of God's two most familiar Scriptures about "wings" are:

"He who dwells in the secret place of the Most High shall abide under the shadow of the Almighty. ² I will say of the Lord, 'He is my refuge and my fortress; My God, in Him I will trust.' ³ Surely He shall deliver you from the snare of the fowler And from the perilous pestilence. ⁴ He shall cover you with His feathers, And under His <u>wings</u> you shall take refuge; His truth shall be your shield and buckler. ⁵ You shall not be afraid of the terror by night, Nor of the arrow that flies by day, ⁶ Nor of the pestilence that walks in darkness, Nor of the destruction that lays waste at noonday. ⁷ A thousand may fall at your side, And ten thousand at your right hand; But it shall not come near you. ⁸ Only with your eyes shall you look, And see the reward of the wicked. ⁹ Because you have made the Lord, who is my refuge, Even the Most High, your dwelling place, ¹⁰ No evil shall befall you, Nor shall any plague come near your dwelling; ¹¹ For He shall give His angels charge over you, To keep you in all your ways. ¹² In their <u>hands</u> [KAF] they shall bear you up, Lest you dash your foot against a stone" (Psalms 91:1-12 _{Additions in brackets mine}).

"¹ 'For behold, the day is coming, Burning like an oven, And all the proud, yes, all who do wickedly will be stubble. And the day which is coming shall burn them up,' Says the Lord of hosts, 'That will leave them neither root nor branch. ² But to you who fear My name the Sun of Righteousness shall arise with healing in His <u>wings</u>; And you shall go out And grow fat like stall-fed calves. ³ You shall trample the wicked, For they shall be ashes under the soles of your feet On the day that I do this,' Says the Lord of hosts" (Malachi 4:1-3).

There are also the wings of the Cherubim on the Ark of the Covenant, which is the way God chose to manifest His Presence to Israel after the sin of the Golden Calf.

"¹⁸ And you shall make two cherubim of gold; of hammered work you shall make them at the two ends of the mercy seat. ¹⁹ Make one cherub at one end, and the other cherub at the other end; you shall make the cherubim at the two ends of it of one piece with the mercy seat. ²⁰ And the cherubim shall stretch out their <u>wings</u> above, covering the mercy seat with their <u>wings</u>, and they shall face one another; the faces of the cherubim shall be toward the mercy seat. ²¹ You shall put the mercy seat on top of the Ark, and in the Ark you shall put the Testimony that I will give you. ²² And there I will meet with you, and I will speak with you from above the mercy seat, from between the two cherubim which are on the Ark of the Testimony, about everything which I will give you in commandment to the children of Israel" (Exodus 25:18-22). The Psalmist Asaph penned this: *"Give ear, O Shepherd of Israel, You who lead Joseph like a flock; You who dwell between the cherubim, shine forth!" (Psalms 80:1).*

The noise of the wings of the four living creatures (Cherubim) is said to be the voice of the Almighty.

> *"²² The likeness of the firmament above the heads of the living creatures was like the color of an awesome crystal, stretched out over their heads. ²³ And under the firmament their <u>wings</u> spread out straight, one toward another. Each one had two which covered one side, and each one had two which covered the other side of the body. ²⁴ When they went, I heard the noise of their <u>wings</u>, like the noise of many waters, <u>like the voice of the Almighty</u>, a tumult like the noise of an army; and when they stood still, they let down their <u>wings</u>. ²⁵ A voice came from above the firmament that was over their heads; whenever they stood, they let down their <u>wings</u>" (Ezekiel 1:22-25).*

Additionally, there is a form of a man's hand (KAF) under the cherubim's wings [*kanaph* in Hebrew] and their wings are full of eyes.

> *" ⁵ And the <u>sound of the wings of the cherubim</u> was heard even in the outer court, <u>like the voice of Almighty God</u> when He speaks. ⁶ Then it happened, when He commanded the man clothed in linen, saying, 'Take fire from among the wheels from among the cherubim,' that he went in and stood beside the wheels. ⁷ And the cherub stretched out his hand from among the cherubim to the fire that was among the cherubim, and took some of it and put it into the hands of the man clothed with linen, who took it and went out. ⁸ The cherubim appeared to have the <u>form of a man's hand under their wings</u>. ⁹ And when I looked, there were four wheels by the cherubim, one wheel by one cherub and another wheel by each other cherub; the wheels appeared to have the color of a beryl stone. ¹⁰ As for their appearance, all four looked alike—as it were, a wheel in the middle of a wheel. ¹¹ When they went, they went toward any of their four directions; they did not turn aside when they went, but followed in the direction the head was facing. They did not turn aside when they went. ¹² And their whole body, with their back, their hands, their <u>wings</u>, and the wheels that the four had, were full of eyes all around" (Ezekiel:10:5-12).*

There are three Hebrew letters that compose the Hebrew word for "king" (מֶלֶךְ). *Melech* is made up of KAF (כ), LAMED (ל), and MEM (מ). Notice how they appear in reverse alphabetic order, which represents the attribute of judgment. It is a monarch's responsibility to maintain law and order in their kingdom. Significantly, when the kings of the dynasty of *David ha Melech* (King David) were anointed, special oil was smeared on their heads in the shape of the letter KAF (כ). The Hebrew letter KAF (כ) represents a crown (כֶּתֶר).

Since KAF's (כ) pictograph looks like the palm of a hand (anything contained in the palm of a hand) or a wing, it represents the place in the body where the potential is actualized. The two Hebrew letters that spell KAF (כף) are the initial letters of two Hebrew words *koach* ("potential") and *poel* ("actual"); therefore, KAF hints at the latent power within the spiritual realm of the potential to fully manifest in the physical realm—the actual.

Grammatically, when a Hebrew word is prefixed with a KAF (כ), it carries the meaning being "like" or "as." When we "prefix" ourselves with the KAF (כ) of the Messiah, we are conformed to His image. We resemble Him, specifically, we resemble Yeshua in what we do. The Havdalah blessing at the conclusion of the Sabbath and festivals refers to the transition from holy activities (Sabbath) to normal activities (weekdays). To indicate the difference between the two, a person opens and closes their hand near the multi-wicked candlelight. The open hand symbolizes the work-free rest of the out-going Sabbath while the closed hand signifies the readiness for action and acquisition. ²⁸

---

²⁸ *The Wisdom of the Hebrew Alphabet* by Rabbi Michael L. Munk, p. 135

The Way Of Wisdom

1. What is a potential in your life that you would like to see actualized?

_____

_____

_____

_____

_____

2. How can you point your wings to kingdom life and action?

_____

_____

_____

_____

_____

3. Believers in the Lord and Savior Jesus Christ are commissioned into the Order of Melchizedek, as kings and priests, when they enter the Kingdom of God. Research the phrase "enter the Kingdom of God" in Scripture. The following are a few references:

Born of water and the Spirit (John 3:5-6). _____

_____

_____

Through many tribulations (Acts 14:22). _____

_____

_____

Receive it like a child (Mark 10:15). _____

_____

_____

It's hard for those who trust in riches (Mark 10:23-25). _____

_____

_____

4. What are some ways you can be prefixed with the KAF (כ) of the Messiah where you are conformed to His image? See Romans 8:29, 12:2; Philippians 3:10; 1 Peter 1:14.

_____

_____

_____

_____

_____

5. Further break down your understanding of the "palms of My hands" in Isaiah 49:16 by contemplating the other concepts that surround it:

The Lord comforting His people (Isa. 49:13)._____

_____

_____

God will not forget you (Isa. 49:15). _____

_____

_____

Our walls are continually before Him (Isa. 49:16)._____

_____

_____

Your destroyers shall go away from you (Isa. 49:17)._____

_____

_____

Others will be gathered together and come to you (Isa. 49:18)._____

_____

_____

6. What encouragement do you receive from knowing that _"all who do wickedly will be as stubble"_ _(Malachi 4:1)_? Notice God says and means "all" the wicked.

_____

_____

_____

7. What comfort do you get from the promise *"But to you who fear My name the Sun of Righteousness shall arise with healing in His wings" (Malachi 4:2)*? Note: The holy reverential fear is an aspect of His glorious love. It enables a person to love what God loves and hate what He hates.

_____

_____

_____

8. Investigate various references to "wings" in Scripture to solidify what you just learned and apply it to your own life.

*"I bore you on eagles' **wings** and brought you to Myself" (Exo. 19:4).* _____

_____

_____

*"The cherubim spread out their **wings** above, and covered the mercy seat with their **wings**. They faced one another; the faces of the cherubim were toward the mercy seat" (Exo. 37:9).*

_____

_____

_____

*"The LORD repay your work, and a full reward be given you by the LORD God of Israel, under whose **wings** you have come for refuge" (Ruth 2:12).* _____

_____

_____

*"Keep me as the apple of Your eye; Hide me under the shadow of Your **wings**" (Psalms 17:8).*

_____

_____

_____

*"Be merciful to me, O God, be merciful to me! For my soul trusts in You; And in the shadow of Your **wings** I will make my refuge, Until these calamities have passed by" (Psalms 57:1).*

_____

_____

_____

*"He shall cover you with His feathers, And under His **wings** you shall take refuge; His truth shall be your shield and buckler" (Psalms 91:4).* _____

_____

_____

KAF (כ)

Which ALEF-TAV (את) facet of KAF (כ) wisdom makes you fly?

PRACTICE WRITING KAF

◆ KAF with a dagesh makes a "k" sound as in "king." Khaf without a dagesh makes a "kh" sound as in "loch." ◆
Start at the top left. With a single stroke draw a backward "c." Then add the dagesh dot in the center.

is the palm of the hand filled with sincerity—KAVANAH (כַּוָּנָה)—which reveals a prayer life of depth and meaning. To kavanah is to pray with purpose and sincerity where your heart and mind are engaged in the act of coming before the King of Kings and the Lord of all Creation. Mindful, sincere prayers happen through ones who focus on what is the good, the pleasing, and the perfect will of the Father. Always remember that prayer is a conversation, so the power of prayer includes listening as well as speaking.

LAMED

WISDOM FOURTEEN

ל
LAMED

LAMED (ל)

LAMED (ל) is the twelfth *Hebrew Living™ Letter* of the Alef-Bet whose pronunciation is *lah-med*. LAMED (ל) has an ordinal value of 12 and a numerical value of 30, which means that the Hebrews can use it for either the number 12 or 30.

The ancient pictograph for LAMED (ל) agrees with the meaning of its name. In ancient Hebrew LAMED means a cattle goad or a shepherd's staff/rod. Its pictograph of a rod symbolizes controlling, prodding, urging forward, going toward, or a tongue. [29]

LAMED (ל) IN ALEF-TAV (את)

You and I can personally choose to engage the essence of Messiah Yeshua—the Word of God—contained within the Hebrew letter LAMED (ל). The ALEF-TAV (את) redemption for LAMED (ל) focuses on Messiah Yeshua proclaiming twice during the Feast of Dedication "I am the Good Shepherd":

> *"I am the Good Shepherd; a good shepherd risks his life for the sake of his sheep. But the hired person who is not the shepherd and who is not the owner of the sheep, when he sees the wolf coming, leaves the sheep and runs away; and the world comes and seizes and scatters the sheep. The hired person runs away because he is hired and does not care for the sheep. I am the Good Shepherd, and I know my own, and my own know me" (John 10:11-14* Lamsa's Aramaic *).*

The passage from John 8:12 to John 10:42 portrays Yeshua during the Feast of Dedication (Hanukkah). Every reference to "shepherd" in the Word of God is connected to the two *"I am the Good Shepherd"* statements that Yeshua made during this feast focused on the dedication or re-dedication of one's heart.

One of my favorite verses about Messiah Yeshua being our Good Shepherd is founded in the Book of Hebrews. When Abraham got his new name, he is first called *"Abraham the Hebrew" (Genesis 14:13)*.

> *"Now may the God of peace [Who is the Author and the Giver of peace], Who brought again from the dead our Lord Jesus, that Great Shepherd of the sheep, by the Blood [that sealed, ratified] the everlasting agreement (covenant, testament), strengthen (complete, perfect) and make you what you ought to be and equip you with everything good that you may carry out His will; [while He Himself] works in you and accomplishes that which is pleasing in His sight, through Jesus Christ (the Messiah); to Whom be the glory forever and ever (to the ages of the ages) Amen (so be it)" (Hebrews 13:20-21* Amplified *).*

---

[29] *Hebrew Word Pictures* by Frank T. Seekins, Lamed, p. 56

Our Great Shepherd ALEF-TAV (את) gave us the most excellent example of how we can follow in His footsteps.

> *"This is the kind of life you've been invited into, the kind of life Christ lived. He suffered everything that came his way so you would know that it could be done, and also know how to do it, step-by-step. He never did one thing wrong, Not once said anything amiss. They called him every name in the book and he said nothing back. He suffered in silence, content to let God set things right. He used His servant body to carry our sins to the Cross so we could be rid of sin, free to live the right way. His wounds became your healing. You were lost sheep with no idea who you were or where you were going. Now you're named and kept for good by the Shepherd of your souls" (1 Peter 2:21-25_{MSG}).*

> *"He shall feed his flock like a shepherd . . . gather the lambs with his arm, and carry them in his bosom, and . . . gently lead those that are young" (Isaiah 40:11).*

When God asks, "Who is the shepherd that will stand before me?" He is inquiring, Who will love my lambs as I do? Who will move with the cadences of My heart to love and teach the sheep that appears to have no shepherd? Our Good Shepherd restores our souls and leads us in the paths of righteousness for His Name's sake (Psalm 23:3) so that we can dwell in the House of the Lord forever (Psalm 23:6).

1 Peter 5:4 tells us when the Chief Shepherd appears, we shall receive a crown of glory that fades not.

> *"² Shepherd the flock of God which is among you, serving as overseers, not by compulsion but willingly, not for dishonest gain but eagerly; ³ nor as being lords over those entrusted to you, but being examples to the flock; ⁴ and when the Chief Shepherd appears, you will receive the crown of glory that does not fade away" (1 Peter 5:2-4).*

Behold, in the midst of God's Kingdom is a lamb who is in the midst of the Throne who will shepherd all of God's people by leading them to the fountains of living water, fresh-tender green pastures, and a table in the presence of your enemies where you will feast on His goodness (Psalms 23; Revelation 7:17).

Thoughts

Listen closely little lambs. Put your head on His bosom and hear His heart, for His rod will protect you, and His staff will truly guide and comfort you (Psalm 23:4).

LAMED (ל) is a unique and majestic Hebrew letter that towers above the other letters from its position in the heart of the Hebrew Alphabet. Since LAMED (ל) towers over the other letters from its central position, it is said to represent *melekh hamelakhim*—the King of Kings. It is not a coincidence that the three central letters of the Hebrew Alef-bet can spell out the Hebrew word *melech* (מלך), which means king. *"These will make war with the Lamb, and the Lamb will overcome them, for <u>He is Lord of lords and King of kings</u>; and those who are with Him are called, chosen, and faithful" (Revelation 17:14).*

> ***"Now out of His mouth goes a sharp sword, that with it He should strike the nations. And He Himself will rule them with a rod of iron. He Himself treads the winepress of the fierceness and wrath of Almighty God. And He has on His robe and on His thigh a name written: <u>King of Kings and Lord of Lords</u>" (Revelation 19:15-16).***

The Hebrew name for the letter itself—LAMED (למד)—comes from the root *lamad,* which means to teach or to learn. The first occurrence of *lamad* (למד) in Scripture is in Deuteronomy 4:1.

> ***"Now, O Israel, listen to the statutes and the judgments which I <u>teach</u> you to observe, that you may live, and go in and possess the land which the Lord God of your fathers is giving you" (Deuteronomy 4:1).***

LAMED (למד) can be seen as an acronym for the phrase *lev meivin da-at,* which is translated as "a heart that understands knowledge." In other words, the goal of learning and teaching—LAMED (ל)—is to absorb the lessons into one's heart. And since LAMED ascends over the other Hebrew letters, it represents the prominence of learning and understanding to the heart.

The heart—*lev* (לֵב)—is the center of a man's body, just as LAMED (ל) is the center of the Hebrew Alphabet. The Hebrew Word Picture for *"lev"* tells us that the heart is what controls the inside. Just as the heart sustains the body, so does heartfelt learning of the Word of God sustain the spirit. Just as faith without works is dead (James 2:20), so is learning without action: *"Even a child is known by his deeds, whether what he does is pure and right" (Proverbs 20:11).* Studying is not the ultimate goal; but rather, the actions that result from one's study.

Thoughts

The Way Of Wisdom

1. How can you better connect to the Good Shepherd of your soul? Hint: Psalms 23.

_____

_____

_____

2. Why is the majesty of the King of Kings hidden within the kindness of the Chief Shepherd?

_____

_____

_____

3. What are your thoughts about the LAMED (ל)'s prominence of learning through understanding something in one's heart? What is the ultimate goal of this type of study?

_____

_____

_____

4. What makes a good shepherd versus a bad shepherd (John 10:11-18; Zech. 11:15-17)?

_____

_____

_____

5. What messages do you receive when you study various Scriptures that contain "shepherd"?

_____

_____

_____

_____

"The LORD is my **shepherd**; I shall not want" (Psa. 23:1). _____

_____

_____

_____

"Save Your people, And bless Your inheritance; **Shepherd** them also, And bear them up forever" (Psa. 28:9).

_____

_____

_____

"He also chose David His servant, And took him from the sheepfolds; ⁷¹ From following the ewes that had young He brought him, To **shepherd** Jacob His people, And Israel His inheritance. ⁷² So he **shepherd**ed them according to the integrity of his heart, And guided them by the skillfulness of his hands" (Psa. 78:70-72).

_____

_____

_____

"He will feed His flock like a **shepherd**; He will gather the lambs with His arm, And carry them in His bosom, And gently lead those who are with young" (Isa. 40:11).

_____

_____

_____

"And I will give you **shepherd**s according to My heart, who will feed you with knowledge and understanding" (Jer. 3:15).

_____

_____

_____

" 'Woe to the **shepherd**s who destroy and scatter the sheep of My pasture!' says the LORD" (Jer. 23:1).

_____

_____

_____

"All the nations will be gathered before Him, and He will separate them one from another, as a **shepherd** divides his sheep from the goats" (Matt. 25:32).

_____

_____

_____

*"Now may the God of peace who brought up our Lord Jesus from the dead, that great **Shepherd** of the sheep, through the blood of the everlasting covenant, ²¹ make you complete in every good work to do His will, working in you what is well pleasing in His sight, through Jesus Christ, to whom be glory forever and ever. Amen"* (Heb. 13:20-21).

_____

_____

_____

_____

*"For you were like sheep going astray, but have now returned to the **Shepherd** and Overseer of your souls"* (1 Pet. 2:25).

_____

_____

_____

6.   Study the LAMED (ל) references to shepherd's "staff":

David took his **staff** in his hand; and chose five smooth stones from the brook, and put them in his shepherd's bag (1 Sam. 17:40).

_____

_____

_____

God's rod and **staff** comfort His people (Psa. 23:4).

_____

_____

_____

The LORD breaks the **staff** of the wicked, which is the scepter of the rulers (Isa. 14:5).

_____

_____

_____

By faith, Jacob worshiped leaning on the top of his **staff** when he was dying (Heb. 11:21).

_____

_____

_____

7. Study the LAMED (לְ) references to shepherd's "rod":

*"You shall take this **rod** in your hand, with which you shall do the signs" (Exo. 4:17).*

_____

_____

_____

*"Lift up your **rod**, and stretch out your hand over the sea and divide it. And the children of Israel shall go on dry ground through the midst of the sea" (Exo. 14:16).*

_____

_____

_____

*"And Moses said to Joshua, 'Choose us some men and go out, fight with Amalek. Tomorrow I will stand on the top of the hill with the **rod** of God in my hand' " (Exo. 17:9).*

_____

_____

_____

*"Now it came to pass on the next day that Moses went into the tabernacle of witness, and behold, the **rod** of Aaron, of the house of Levi, had sprouted and put forth buds, had produced blossoms and yielded ripe almonds" (Num. 17:8).*

_____

_____

_____

*"The LORD shall send the **rod** of Your strength out of Zion. Rule in the midst of Your enemies!" (Psa. 110:2).*

_____

_____

_____

*"Now gather yourself in troops, O daughter of troops; He has laid siege against us; They will strike the judge of Israel with a **rod** on the cheek" (Micah 5:1).*

_____

_____

_____

*"Violence has risen up into a **rod** of wickedness" (Ezek. 7:11).*

_____

_____

_____

LAMED (ל)

What is your favorite LAMED (ל) wisdom gem that you picked up about
ALEF-TAV (את) being the Good Shepherd?

PRACTICE WRITING LAMED

● Pronounced as *lah-med* ●

Start at the top left above the line to draw a short line straight down.

Then continue by drawing a horizontal line to the right until curving downward to the bottom line.

ל

is tall and beautiful and is the
heart—LEV (לֵב)—of the
Good Shepherd who offers a
resting place in His luxurious love
and guides His flock to an
oasis of peace.

MEM

WISDOM FIFTEEN

מ

MEM

MEM (מ)

MEM (מ) is the thirteenth *Hebrew Living™ Letter* of the Alef-Bet whose pronunciation *mem* is with the sound of "m" as in mom. MEM (מ) has an ordinal value of 13 and a numerical value of 40, which means that the Hebrews can use it for either the number 13 or 40.

The ancient pictograph for MEM (מ) agrees with the meaning of its name. In ancient Hebrew MEM means water. The picture of waves can be seen for the ancient MEM symbol. This pictograph symbolizes water; mighty, massive, or many (like the ocean); chaos (like a turbulent ocean); and to come from (like water down a stream or river). [30]

MEM (מ) IN ALEF-TAV (את)

You and I can personally choose to engage the essence of Messiah Yeshua—the Word of God—contained within the Hebrew letter MEM (מ). The ALEF-TAV (את) redemption for MEM (מ) focuses on Messiah Yeshua as the pure source of living water.

> "*7 A woman of Samaria came to draw water. Jesus said to her, 'Give Me a drink.' 8 For His disciples had gone away into the city to buy food. 9 Then the woman of Samaria said to Him, 'How is it that You, being a Jew, ask a drink from me, a Samaritan woman?' For Jews have no dealings with Samaritans. 10 Jesus answered and said to her, 'If you knew the gift of God, and who it is who says to you, "Give Me a drink," you would have asked Him, and He would have given you living water.' 11 The woman said to Him, 'Sir, You have nothing to draw with, and the well is deep. Where then do You get that living water? 12 Are You greater than our father Jacob, who gave us the well, and drank from it himself, as well as his sons and his livestock?' 13 Jesus answered and said to her, 'Whoever drinks of this water will thirst again, 14 but whoever drinks of the water that I shall give him will never thirst. But the water that I shall give him will become in him a fountain of water springing up into everlasting life' *" (John 4:7-14).

> "*And Jesus said to them, 'I am the bread of life. He who comes to Me shall never hunger, and he who believes in Me shall never thirst' *" (John 6:35).

---

[30] *Hebrew Word Pictures* by Frank T. Seekins, Mem, p. 60

Behold, in the midst of God's Kingdom is a lamb who is in the midst of the Throne who will shepherd and lead all of God's people to the fountains of living water.

" ⁹After these things I looked, and behold, a great multitude which no one could number, of all nations, tribes, peoples, and tongues, standing before the throne and before the Lamb, clothed with white robes, with palm branches in their hands, ¹⁰and crying out with a loud voice, saying, 'Salvation belongs to our God who sits on the throne, and to the Lamb!' ¹¹All the angels stood around the throne and the elders and the four living creatures, and fell on their faces before the throne and worshiped God, ¹²saying: 'Amen! Blessing and glory and wisdom, Thanksgiving and honor and power and might, Be to our God forever and ever. Amen.' ¹³Then one of the elders answered, saying to me, 'Who are these arrayed in white robes, and where did they come from?' ¹⁴And I said to him, 'Sir, you know.' So he said to me, 'These are the ones who come out of the great tribulation, and washed their robes and made them white in the blood of the Lamb. ¹⁵Therefore they are before the throne of God, and serve Him day and night in His temple. And He who sits on the throne will dwell among them. ¹⁶They shall neither hunger anymore nor thirst anymore; the sun shall not strike them, nor any heat; ¹⁷for the Lamb who is in the midst of the throne will shepherd them and lead them to <u>living fountains of waters</u>. And God will wipe away every tear from their eyes' " (Revelation 7:9-17).

On the seventh day of the Feast of Tabernacles *(Sukkot)* Yeshua spoke of His living water: *"On the last day, that great day of the feast, Jesus stood and cried out, saying, 'If anyone thirsts, let him come to Me and drink. He who believes in Me, as the Scripture has said, out of his heart will flow rivers of <u>living water</u>' " (John 7:37-38).*

The Hebrews have been told: "He who has not seen the rejoicing at the place of the water-drawing has never seen rejoicing in his life." The water pouring became a focus of the joy that the Torah commands for *Sukkot*. On no other festival were the people literally commanded to be joyful. As a result, *Sukkot* became known as "the season of our joy," just as Passover is "the season of our freedom."

The water pouring ceremony at the Feast of Tabernacles was the only water poured out onto God's altar. This water was literally called "Yeshua"—the waters of salvation. Jesus proclaimed *"If anyone drinks of Me"* in God's Temple, which demonstrated that He was (and He still is) these waters of salvation. This was the very place where Peter preached on the day of Pentecost (Acts 2). It was also the place where the Rabbis used to teach about the coming Messiah.

Thoughts

As we have discussed, MEM (מ) represents water. The Hebrew word for water is *mayim*, which has a plural ending. God founded our physical world on the waters:

> *"The earth is the Lord's, and all its fullness, The world and those who dwell therein. For He has founded it upon the seas, And established it upon the waters" (Psalms 24:1-2).*

Righteousness is equated to the security of life-giving water. Psalms 1:3 compares a righteous man to a tree securely planted beside channels of water.

> *"Blessed is the man who walks not in the counsel of the ungodly, Nor stands in the path of sinners, Nor sits in the seat of the scornful; But his delight is in the law of the Lord, And in His law he meditates day and night. He shall be like a tree planted by the rivers of water, That brings forth its fruit in its season, whose leaf also shall not wither; and whatever he does shall prosper" (Psalms 1:1-3).*

After the LORD speaks of the fast that He chooses, God promises to satisfy a person's soul in drought, like a spring of water whose waters do not fail: *"The Lord will guide you continually, and satisfy your soul in drought, and strengthen your bones; you shall be like a watered garden, and like a spring of water, whose waters do not fail" (Isaiah 58:11).*

The LORD brings water into the mix when He speaks of His people forsaking and neglecting Him. *"For My people have committed two evils: they have forsaken Me, the fountain of living waters, and hewn themselves cisterns—broken cisterns that can hold no water" (Jeremiah 2:13).*

How significant that life-giving water is a major theme in the Lord's vindication of Zion.

> *" 'Rejoice with Jerusalem, and be glad with her, all you who love her; rejoice for joy with her, all you who mourn for her; ¹¹ That you may feed and be satisfied with the consolation of her bosom, that you may drink deeply and be delighted with the abundance of her glory.' ¹² For thus says the Lord: 'Behold, I will extend peace to her like a river, and the glory of the Gentiles like a flowing stream. Then you shall feed; on her sides shall you be carried, and be dandled on her knees. ¹³ As one whom his mother comforts, so I will comfort you; and you shall be comforted in Jerusalem' " (Isaiah 66:10-13).*

Thoughts

The Way Of Wisdom

1. How do you keep the water within you pure?

_____

_____

_____

2. Just as the physical world has been founded on waters, so is the spiritual world founded on the Father's love. What are some wonderful realities of water and the Father's love?

_____

_____

_____

3. Research the Biblical references for "living water".

*"For My people have committed two evils: They have forsaken Me, the fountain of **living waters**, And hewn themselves cisterns—broken cisterns that can hold no **water**" (Jer. 2:13).*

_____

_____

_____

*"O LORD, the hope of Israel, All who forsake You shall be ashamed. 'Those who depart from Me Shall be written in the earth, Because they have forsaken the LORD, The fountain of **living waters**'" (Jer. 17:13).*

_____

_____

_____

*"Jesus answered and said to her, 'If you knew the gift of God, and who it is who says to you, "Give Me a drink," you would have asked Him, and He would have given you **living water**.' ¹¹ The woman said to Him, 'Sir, You have nothing to draw with, and the well is deep. Where then do You get that **living water**?'" (John 4:10-11).*

_____

_____

_____

*"He who believes in Me, as the Scripture has said, out of his heart will flow rivers of **living water**"* *(John 7:38).*

_____

_____

_____

4. Research the Biblical references for "Water of Life."

Revelation 21:6: _____

_____

_____

Revelation 22:1: _____

_____

_____

Revelation 22:17: _____

_____

_____

5. Dig a deeper well into "water" by dipping into the Biblical references for "river" or "rivers."

A **river** went out of Eden to water the garden (Gen. 2:10). _____

_____

_____

To those who trust Him, God gives them drink from the **river** of His pleasure (Psa. 36:8).

_____

_____

_____

There is a **river** whose streams make glad the city of God (Psa. 46:4).

_____

_____

_____

God brought streams out of the rock and caused waters to run down like **rivers** (Psa. 78:16).

_____

_____

_____

YHVH extends peace like a **river** (Isa. 66:12).

_____

_____

_____

A pure **river** of water of life proceeds from the throne of God and of the Lamb (Rev. 22:1).

_____

_____

_____

On either side of the pure **river** of the water of life is the Tree of Life (Rev. 22:2).

_____

_____

_____

6. Dive deeper into the Biblical water references to "fountain" or "fountains."

*"For the LORD your God is bringing you into a good land, a land of brooks of water, of **fountain**s and springs, that flow out of valleys and hills" (Deut. 8:7).*

_____

_____

_____

*"For with You is the **fountain** of life; In Your light we see light" (Psa. 36:9).*

_____

_____

_____

*"The fear of the LORD is a **fountain** of life, To turn one away from the snares of death" (Prov. 14:27).*

_____

_____

_____

*"The poor and needy seek water, but there is none, Their tongues fail for thirst. I, the LORD, will hear them; I, the God of Israel, will not forsake them. ^{18} I will open rivers in desolate heights, And **fountains** in the midst of the valleys; I will make the wilderness a pool of water, And the dry land springs of water"* (Isa. 41:17-18).

_____

_____

_____

*"And it will come to pass in that day That the mountains shall drip with new wine, The hills shall flow with milk, And all the brooks of Judah shall be flooded with water; A **fountain** shall flow from the house of the LORD And water the Valley of Acacias"* (Joel 3:18).

_____

_____

_____

*"For the Lamb who is in the midst of the throne will shepherd them and lead them to living **fountains** of waters. And God will wipe away every tear from their eyes"* (Rev. 7:17).

_____

_____

_____

*"And He said to me, 'It is done! I am the Alpha and the Omega, the Beginning and the End. I will give of the **fountain** of the water of life freely to him who thirsts'"* (Rev. 21:6).

_____

_____

_____

7. You can dive as deep as you desire into other Biblical water references, like "streams," "pools," "rain" etc.

_____

_____

_____

_____

MEM (מ)

What is your most preferred MEM (מ) wisdom stream regarding ALEF-TAV (את) being the Water of Life?

PRACTICE WRITING MEM

♦ Pronounced *mem* with the sound of "m" as in mom ♦

There is a gap at the bottom left of the letter. Start at the bottom left. Draw up and curve around to the top right, then curve around down to the bottom line. Once at the bottom line. Draw a straight line backwards leaving a gap to the left Then add a YUD (׳) to the upper left.

מ מ מ מ מ מ

מ

מ

מ

מ

מ

מ

מ

מ

מ

is the physical substance that
Earth has been founded. This is
the water—MAYIM (מַיִם)—and
this is the wilderness—MIDBAR
(מִדְבָּר)—that we wander
and are made ready to enter
the Promise Land.

WISDOM SIXTEEN

נ
NUN

NUN/NOON (נ)

NUN (נ) is the fourteenth *Hebrew Living™ Letter* of the Alef-Bet whose pronunciation is *noon*. NUN (נ) has an ordinal value of 14 and a numerical value of 50, which means that the Hebrews can use it for either the number 14 or 50.

The ancient pictograph for NUN (נ) agrees with the meaning of its name. In ancient Hebrew NUN means a fish. The picture of a fish darting through water can be seen in the ancient symbols used for NUN (נ). The pictograph for NUN (נ) symbolizes action and life. [31]

NUN (נ) IN ALEF-TAV (את)

You and I can personally choose to engage the essence of Messiah Yeshua—the Word of God—contained within the Hebrew letter NUN (נ). The ALEF-TAV (את) redemption for NUN (נ) focuses on the resurrection of Messiah, which is portrayed in the sign of the Prophet Jonah. Yeshua spoke about Jonah, his experience with the huge fish, and his preaching of repentance to the citizens of Nineveh. Yeshua emphasized the importance of Jonah's experience by saying that the only sign that would be given to the skeptical, religious people of His day was the sign of Jonah.

> " *38 Then some of the scribes and Pharisees answered, saying, 'Teacher, we want to see a sign from You.' 39 But He answered and said to them, 'An evil and adulterous generation seeks after a sign, and no sign will be given to it except the <u>sign of the prophet Jonah</u>. 40 For as Jonah was three days and three nights in the belly of the great fish, so will the Son of Man be three days and three nights in the heart of the earth. 41 The men of Nineveh will rise up in the judgment with this generation and condemn it, because they repented at the preaching of Jonah; and indeed a greater than Jonah is here' " (Matthew 12:38-41).*

Why would Yeshua say the *"an evil and adulterous generation seeks after a sign" (Matt. 12:39)*? I am sure that there are more than one answer to this question. What comes to mind is the verse *"For false christs and false prophets will rise and show great signs and wonders to deceive, if possible, even the elect" (Matthew 24:24)*. This is such a sobering thought! Even though signs, wonders, and miracles are supposed to follow those who believe (Mark 16:17), lying signs and wonders according to the working of Satan accompany the Antichrist, i.e., the "lawless one" (2 Thess. 2:9-10). Therefore, we are not to focus on the signs, miracles, and wonders; but on Messiah Yeshua who fulfilled the sign of Jonah. And, it is always wise to test the spirit at work when any sign and wonder is demonstrated: *"Every spirit that confesses that Jesus Christ has come in the flesh is of God" (1 John 4:2)*.

---

[31] *Hebrew Word Pictures* by Frank T. Seekins, Noon, p. 64

If you are unsure if something is of God, or not; first, take your own thoughts and desires captive to the obedience of Christ by choosing to let go of them and lay them on God's Altar (2 Cor. 10:5). [32] Since the idols of your own heart can sound so much like God's voice that it can be almost indistinguishable, it is wise to also take dominion and authority over all known and unknown idols by the Blood of the Lamb before you ask the Lord a question. You can also add a dangerous prayer: "Lord, I side with You, even against myself," if you truly want to be set free (John 8:32). Then, after you hear what you believe is Yeshua/Father's answer, test the spirits. I pray something like: "Love, I believe I heard such-and-such. I want to test the spirit of this answer by asking if this spirit confesses that Jesus Christ (Messiah Yeshua) came in the flesh, was born of a virgin, died on the Cross, and rose again in three days." I add those details to give myself time to settle down to hear properly. That's when a person will hear, either "yes," or "no," or "maybe." The only correct answer is "yes." If you hear static, keep pressing in (asking and seeking) until you know that you know that it's Yeshua and the Father speaking.

The Hebrew word for "sign" in "the sign of the Prophet Jonah" is *oth*. It means a signal, a beacon, a monument, evidence, or proof. Yeshua was, and is, saying: Here's your sign! *"For as Jonah was three days and three nights in the belly of the great fish, so will the Son of Man be three days and three nights in the heart of the earth" (Matthew 12:40).* Here's the beacon of hope. Here's the monument for the ages. Here is evidence of eternal life. Here is the proof of resurrection and a greater ministry than Jonah.

> *" 8 For He was cut off from the land of the living; For the transgressions of My people He was stricken. 9 And they made His grave with the wicked—But with the rich at His death, Because He had done no violence, Nor was any deceit in His mouth. 10 Yet it pleased the Lord to bruise Him; He has put Him to grief. When You make His soul an offering for sin, He shall see His seed, He shall prolong His days, And the pleasure of the Lord shall prosper in His hand. 11 He shall see the labor of His soul, and be satisfied. By His knowledge My righteous Servant shall justify many, For He shall bear their iniquities. 12 Therefore I will divide Him a portion with the great, And He shall divide the spoil with the strong, Because He poured out His soul unto death, And He was numbered with the transgressors, And He bore the sin of many, And made intercession for the transgressors" (Isaiah 53:8-12).*

Notice that Father God (Abba) made Yeshua's soul an offering for sin. Abba saw the labor of Yeshua's soul and was/is satisfied. And, Messiah Yeshua incredibly poured out His soul unto death bearing the sins of the world, being numbered with the transgressors. Through the Pattern Son's mind-blowing soul work, a way was made to reconnect the Seven Spirits of God in mankind's body, soul, and spirit, so each of us can follow the Messiah's blueprint which will enable us to return back to Eden and beyond.

One of Yeshua's famous "I am" statements is "I am the Resurrection and the Life."

> *" 25 Jesus said to her [Martha], 'I am the Resurrection and the Life. He who believes in Me, though he may die, he shall live. 26 And whoever lives and believes in Me shall never die. Do you believe this?' 27 She said to Him, 'Yes, Lord, I believe that You are the Christ, the Son of God, who is to come into the world'" (John 11:25-27 Addition in brackets mine).*

The first mention of the word "nun" is in *Exodus 33:11* in reference to Joshua, the son of Nun:

> *"So the Lord spoke to Moses face to face, as a man speaks to his friend. And he would return to the camp, but his servant Joshua the son of <u>Nun</u>, a young man, did not depart from the Tabernacle."* Joshua succeeded Moses and was able to enter the Promised Land,

---
[32] *Victory Over Crucified Thoughts* by Robin Main. https://sapphirethroneministries.wordpress.com/2013/10/27/victory-over-uncrucified-thoughts/

as the Son of Life. *"After the death of Moses the servant of the Lord, it came to pass that the Lord spoke to Joshua the son of Nun, Moses' assistant, saying: ² 'Moses My servant is dead. Now therefore, arise, go over this Jordan, you and all this people, to the land which I am giving to them—the children of Israel. ³ Every place that the sole of your foot will tread upon I have given you, as I said to Moses' "* (Joshua 1:1-3).

NUN (נ) has two forms. The bent (נ) is used at the beginning or middle of a word while the elongated (ן) is used at the end of a word. NUN (נ) stands for the reliable and faithful one while NUN (ן) denotes continuity. The most faithful one is God Himself. *"Your mercy, O Lord, is in the heavens; Your faithfulness reaches to the clouds"* (Psalms 36:5). [33] God's faithfulness can be emulated by humans. A person may be like a bent NUN whose heart is humble, serving in veneration and awe. Or, they may be like the erect NUN who serves God with a steadfast heart of love, full of unwavering faith. [34] "On the Day of Judgment, the person's own soul will testify before God" (Rashi), as it is written: The soul of man is the candle of HASHEM, searching all the inward parts (Proverbs 20:27). [35]

Since NUN (נ) is a picture of a fish darting through water, which symbolizes action and life, we can connect Scriptures that contain the words "fish," "action," and "life." As Yeshua walked by the Sea of Galilee, He called out to Peter and his brother Andrew: *"Follow Me, and I will make you fishers of men"* (Matthew 4:19). They immediately left their fishing nets and followed Him.

Once Yeshua paid the ultimate price on the cross, His disciples momentarily went back to the water and its provision of fish. God met them there. This is the third time Yeshua appeared to His disciples after His Resurrection.

" ³ Simon Peter said to them, 'I am going fishing.' They said to him, 'We are going with you also.' They went out and immediately got into the boat, and that night they caught nothing. ⁴ But when the morning had now come, Jesus stood on the shore; yet the disciples did not know that it was Jesus. ⁵ Then Jesus said to them, 'Children, have you any food?' They answered Him, 'No.' ⁶ And He said to them, 'Cast the net on the right side of the boat, and you will find some.' So they cast, and now they were not able to draw it in because of the multitude of fish. ⁷ Therefore that disciple whom Jesus loved said to Peter, 'It is the Lord!' Now when Simon Peter heard that it was the Lord, he put on his outer garment (for he had removed it), and plunged into the sea. ⁸ But the other disciples came in the little boat (for they were not far from land, but about two hundred cubits), dragging the net with fish. ⁹ Then, as soon as they had come to land, they saw a fire of coals there, and fish laid on it, and bread. ¹⁰ Jesus said to them, 'Bring some of the fish which you have just caught.' ¹¹ Simon Peter went up and dragged the net to land, full of large fish, one hundred and fifty-three; and although there were so many, the net was not broken" (John 21:3-11).

What was the secret of the overflowing abundant provision of 153 large fish? The secret of the 153 fish resides with the King of Kings who calls the fishermen to cast their net (the Gospel of the Kingdom) on the right side to bring the people out of the nations (sea of humanity). The phrase "the sons of God" in Hebrew is equivalent to 153. Also, eleven times throughout the Torah, the number 153 is connected to the word *HaPesach*, the Passover, and His peoples' Exodus out of the world. When all the numbers from 1 to 17 are added together, they equal 153; thus this number can represent all those who believe and obey or all those who cast their net on the right side (Heb. 5:9).

---

[33] *The Wisdom of the Hebrew Alphabet* by Rabbi Michael L. Munk, p. 151
[34] *The Wisdom of the Hebrew Alphabet* by Rabbi Michael L. Munk, p. 152
[35] *The Wisdom of the Hebrew Alphabet* by Rabbi Michael L. Munk, p. 153

The Way Of Wisdom

1. Why do you think that Yeshua said that the only sign to be given to the Scribes and Pharisees is the sign of Jonah?

_____

_____

_____

2. What are your thoughts about Yeshua saying *"an evil and adulterous generation seeks after a sign"* *(Matt. 12:39)*?

_____

_____

_____

3. Investigate the word "sign" in Scripture to seek to further understand Yeshua's warning. Notice how many of the God-given signs have been twisted from their original Biblical meaning by the world and by the religious.

*"Then God said, 'Let there be lights in the firmament of the heavens to divide the day from the night; and let them be for **sign**s and seasons, and for days and years'" (Gen. 1:14).*

_____

_____

_____

*"And God said to Noah, 'This is the **sign** of the covenant which I have established between Me and all flesh that is on the earth'" (Gen. 9:17).*

_____

_____

_____

*"Now the blood shall be a **sign** for you on the houses where you are. And when I see the blood, I will pass over you; and the plague shall not be on you to destroy you when I strike the land of Egypt" (Exo. 12:13).*

_____

_____

_____

_____

*"It is a **sign** between Me and the children of Israel forever; for in six days the L*ORD* made the heavens and the earth, and on the seventh day He rested and was refreshed" (Exo. 31:17).*

_____

_____

_____

*"Because all these men who have seen My glory and the **signs** which I did in Egypt and in the wilderness, and have put Me to the test now these ten times, and have not heeded My voice, [23] they certainly shall not see the land of which I swore to their fathers, nor shall any of those who rejected Me see it" (Num. 14:22-23).*

_____

_____

_____

*"And these **signs** will follow those who believe: In My name they will cast out demons; they will speak with new tongues; [18] they will take up serpents; and if they drink anything deadly, it will by no means hurt them; they will lay hands on the sick, and they will recover" (Mark 16:17-18).*

_____

_____

_____

*"Then the beast was captured, and with him the false prophet who worked **signs** in his presence, by which he deceived those who received the mark of the beast and those who worshiped his image. These two were cast alive into the lake of fire burning with brimstone" (Rev. 19:20).*

_____

_____

_____

4. How do you test the spirits (1 John 4:1-4)?

_____

_____

_____

_____

_____

5. What are some ALEF-TAV (את) mentions of NUN (נ) as in "fish"? Please read the Bible verses in context.

After God declares, *"Let Us make man in Our image,"* He first adds *"let them have dominion over the fish of the sea"* (Gen. 1:26).

_____

_____

_____

_____

The **fish** in the Nile River died due to the first plague turning water into blood (Exo. 7:21).

_____

_____

_____

_____

Wherever God's river goes, everything will live, even a great multitude of **fish** (Ezek. 47:9).

_____

_____

_____

_____

YHVH prepared a great **fish** to swallow Jonah (Jonah 1:17).

_____

_____

_____

_____

YHVH spoke to the great **fish**, and it vomited Jonah onto dry land (Jonah 2:10).

_____

_____

_____

_____

Yeshua multiplied five barley loaves and two small **fish** to feed the masses that followed Him (John. 6:8-14).

_____

_____

_____

_____

_____

The flesh of **fish** is different from the flesh of man, animals, and birds (1 Cor. 15:39).

_____

_____

_____

_____

_____

6. Meditate upon the first mention of the word "nun" in _Exodus 33:11_, which is associated with Joshua, the son of Nun, who led God's people into the Promised Land.

_____

_____

_____

_____

_____

7. What are your thoughts about the 153 large fish caught by the disciples after they obeyed the Messiah's instructions? Why do you think Yeshua's third appearance to His disciples after the Resurrection included eating with them on the beach? Hint: Acts 2:42-46.

_____

_____

_____

_____

_____

NUN (נ)

What fresh aspect of wisdom have your learned about the NUN (נ) sign of Jonah for ALEF-TAV (את)?

PRACTICE WRITING NUN

♦ Pronounced *noon* ♦

Start at the top left. Draw the short upper horizontal line to the right, then draw a vertical line down to the bottom line and continue to draw a short horizontal to the left.

נ

is the living soul—N'SHAMAH
(נְשָׁמָה)—that God created in His
own image through the breath of
the Almighty. Each soul—
NEFESH (נֶפֶשׁ)—closes one's
eyes to see the cascading wonders
NIFL'LAOT (נפלאות) of נ. NUN
(נ) is the holy spark—NITZOTZ
(ניצוץ)—in each one of us, which
burns brighter as we are
faithful—NE'EMAN (נֶאֱמָן).

WISDOM SEVENTEEN

ס
SAMECH

SAMECH/SAMEKH (ס)

SAMECH (ס) is the fifteenth *Hebrew Living™ Letter* of the Alef-Bet whose pronunciation is *sah-mekh*. SAMECH (ס) has an ordinal value of 15 and a numerical value of 60, which means that the Hebrews can use it for either the number 15 or 60.

The ancient pictograph for SAMECH (ס) agrees with the meaning of its name. In ancient Hebrew SAMECH means a prop, a support, or an aid. The prop pictograph for SAMECH (ס) symbolizes supporting, a slow twisting (like a plant being changed with a prop), or a turning aside (like a plant). [36]

SAMECH (ס) IN ALEF-TAV (את)

You and I can personally choose to engage the essence of Messiah Yeshua—the Word of God—contained within the Hebrew letter SAMECH (ס). The ALEF-TAV (את) redemption for SAMECH (ס) focuses on the support and strength of Messiah Yeshua as well as Him being an ever-present help. On the active side of SAMECH (ס) God provides support. On the passive side of SAMECH (ס) is a person relying on (trusting) God.

> "*18 Behold, the eye of the Lord is on those who fear Him, On those who hope in His mercy, 19 To deliver their soul from death, And to keep them alive in famine. 20 Our soul waits for the Lord; He is our help and our shield. 21 For our heart shall rejoice in Him, Because we have trusted in His holy name. 22 Let Your mercy, O Lord, be upon us, Just as we hope in You" (Psalms 33:18-22).*

The Lord helps and delivers those who trust in Him.

> "*37 Mark the blameless man, and observe the upright; For the future of that man is peace. 38 But the transgressors shall be destroyed together; The future of the wicked shall be cut off. 39 But the salvation of the righteous is from the Lord; He is their strength in the time of trouble. 40 And the Lord shall help them and deliver them; He shall deliver them from the wicked, And save them, Because they trust in Him" (Psalms 37:37-40).*

---

[36] *Hebrew Word Pictures* by Frank T. Seekins, Samech, p. 68

The Lord is the help and shield of Is-real is repeated three times in Psalms 115, which means it is a complete reality:

> "*⁹ O Israel, <u>trust</u> in the Lord; He is their <u>help</u> and their <u>shield</u>. ¹⁰ O house of Aaron, <u>trust</u> in the Lord; He is their <u>help</u> and their <u>shield</u>. ¹¹ You who fear the Lord, <u>trust</u> in the Lord; He is their <u>help</u> and their <u>shield</u>*" *(Psalms 115:9-11).*

God is right there when you are in trouble.

> "*¹ God is our refuge and strength, <u>A very present help</u> in trouble. ² Therefore we will not fear, Even though the earth be removed, And though the mountains be carried into the midst of the sea; ³ Though its waters roar and be troubled, Though the mountains shake with its swelling. Selah ⁴ There is a river whose streams shall make glad the city of God, The holy place of the tabernacle of the Most High. ⁵ God is in the midst of her, she shall not be moved; God shall <u>help</u> her, just at the break of dawn. ⁶ The nations raged, the kingdoms were moved; He uttered His voice, the earth melted. ⁷ The Lord of hosts is with us; The God of Jacob is our refuge. Selah*" *(Psalms 46:1-7).*

The Lord supports and delivers those He delights in.

> "*¹⁶ He sent from above, He took me; He drew me out of many waters. ¹⁷ He delivered me from my strong enemy, From those who hated me, For they were too strong for me. ¹⁸ They confronted me in the day of my calamity, But <u>the Lord was my support</u>. ¹⁹ He also brought me out into a broad place; He delivered me because He delighted in me. ²⁰ The Lord rewarded me according to my righteousness; According to the cleanness of my hands He has recompensed me. ²¹ For I have kept the ways of the Lord, And have not wickedly departed from my God. ²² For all His judgments were before me, And I did not put away His statutes from me. ²³ I was also blameless before Him, And I kept myself from my iniquity. ²⁴ Therefore the Lord has recompensed me according to my righteousness, According to the cleanness of my hands in His sight. ²⁵ With the merciful You will show Yourself merciful; With a blameless man You will show Yourself blameless; ²⁶ With the pure You will show Yourself pure; And with the devious You will show Yourself shrewd. ²⁷ For You will save the humble people, But will bring down haughty looks. ²⁸ For You will light my lamp; The Lord my God will enlighten my darkness. ²⁹ For by You I can run against a troop, By my God I can leap over a wall. ³⁰ As for God, His way is perfect; The word of the Lord is proven; <u>He is a shield to all who trust in Him</u>*" *(Psalms 18:16-30).*

Some say that the picture of SAMECH (ס) is a shield. Notice how God identifies Himself as Abram's shield:

> "*¹⁸ Then Melchizedek king of Salem brought out bread and wine; he was the priest of God Most High. ¹⁹ And he blessed him and said: 'Blessed be Abram of God Most High, Possessor of heaven and earth; ²⁰ And blessed be God Most High, Who has delivered your enemies into your hand.' And he gave him a tithe of all. ¹ After these things the word of the Lord came to Abram in a vision, saying, 'Do not be afraid, Abram. <u>I am your shield</u>, your exceedingly great reward'*" *(Genesis 14:18-20; Genesis 15:1).*

Before Abram got his name changed, Melchizedek blessed him: *"Blessed be Abram of God Most High, possessor of heaven and earth" (Genesis 14:19)*. If you want to become a fully mature son of the Order of Melchizedek who possesses heaven and earth, you must follow in the footsteps of Abraham. After Abram zealously destroyed all his family's idols as well as the ability to sell and reproduce those idols, Nimrod threw Abram into a fiery furnace many moons before Shadrach, Meshach, and Abednego (Daniel 3).

Abraham's journey is connected to the Kingdom of God while Nimrod is connected to the Kingdom of Self. Both Abram and Nimrod can represent warring factions within each one of us:

> *"For I delight in the law of God after the inward man: but I see another law in my members, warring against the law of my mind, and bringing me into captivity to the law of sin which is in my members" (Romans 7:22-23 $_{KJV}$).*

One chooses to go through the refining process while the other tries to avoid it by throwing others into the scorching fire. After Abram was miraculously rescued from the fire, Abram got a short reprieve from Nimrod's persecution of the worshippers of YHVH. He got a reprieve of one day. The next night Nimrod had a dream, which was interpreted as forecasting Nimrod's defeat by Abram.

The "law of sin" within us (the places in us that are not perfectly aligned with His righteous plumb line) knows that our heavenly man within—*"the law of God after the inward man"*—will be its end. We sometimes fight our need for our daily crucifixion process:

> *"Then He [Yeshua] said to all, 'If anyone desires to come after Me, let him deny himself, and take up his cross daily, and follow Me' " (Luke 9:23 $_{addition\ in\ brackets\ mine}$).*

After the dream, Nimrod plotted to secretly kill Abram, so Abram immigrated to the land of Canaan. Abram's journey illustrates a profound kingdom truth in our day. In this kingdom day, God's people will come out of Babylon . . . out of the fiery furnace from which they emerged after they chose to destroy all their family's idols. After we come out of Babylon, we will temporarily go back into the world (Egypt) where our fear of man will be tested even more. After our sojourn in Egypt, we will return to our Promise Land where we must first conquer the rulership of Babylonian practices and mindsets in our own lives before we can receive the fullness of the ministry of Melchizedek. We must dethrone the same Babylonian kings that Abram did.

Abram naturally and supernaturally overcame four Babylonian kings, which represents the rulership of his entire earth. The meaning of the four names of the Babylonian kings in Genesis 14:1 tells us that we need to overthrow from within the darkness, deception, savagery, mercilessness, false positions, and producing after the Tree of Knowledge of Good and Evil.

Does this mean we conquer those Babylon kings in our genes by His Blood and dethrone them in our life? Yes. This will happen, but I personally believe that we have to recognize our agreement with anything that is earthly, fleshly, or carnal first before we can be transformed. Confession and repentance are huge tools in our restoration to our primordial state, as it was in the beginning before the Fall.

If you will put your hand to the plow and be attentive to His slightest prompting to follow Him to the utmost, HE is the one who knows the way that you need to take in order to come forth as gold (Job 23:10). So, surrender to His process always endeavoring to be in a right and loving relationship first with Him and also with other people. Easier said than done; but keep being faithful choosing to be one with the All-Consuming fire on the Throne and you will overcome . . . be completely one (the exact same essence).

The Hebrew sages say that SAMECH (ס) represents the endless and ever-ascending spiral of God's glory in the universe. His endless cycles are reflected here on earth in the seasons as well as the Biblical Year being marked by the Feasts of the Lord.

The circular form of SAMECH (ס) speaks of the end of something intertwined in its beginning and vice versa. The inherent unity between the end and the beginning is connected to the glorious transcended light of the Most High God, which encompasses every point of reality.

SAMECH (ס) is a closed-rounded Hebrew letter, which represents divine support. Man's confident reliance on God's support is a mainstay of both Judaism and Christianity. It is so fundamental that King Solomon summarizes all of his teachings with the words:

> *"Here now is my final conclusion: Fear God and obey his commands, for this is everyone's duty. God will judge us for everything we do, including every secret thing, whether good or bad" (Ecclesiastes 12:13-14_{NLT}).* [37]

When the Ten Commandments were engraved by the finger of God, the middle of the Hebrew letter SAMECH (ס) had no support; but it miraculously was kept in place and suspended. [38] The perimeter of SAMECH (ס) can represent God—the Protector—while the center of SAMECH (ס) symbolizes what He protects. [39]

> *"I love you, Lord; you are my strength. ² The Lord is my rock, my fortress, and my savior; my God is my rock, <u>in whom I find protection. He is my shield</u>, the power that saves me, and my place of safety" (Psalms 18:1-2_{NLT}).*

---

[37] *The Wisdom of the Hebrew Alphabet* by Rabbi Michael L. Munk, p. 159
[38] *Shabbos 104a*, p. 236
[39] *The Wisdom of the Hebrew Alphabet* by Rabbi Michael L. Munk, p. 160

Thoughts

The Way Of Wisdom

1. What is the benefit of having God as your shield?

_____

_____

_____

2. God identifies Himself as Abram's shield (Gen. 15:1). Look up other references to "shield" in Scripture to see how to properly take up the shield of faith. Here are a few to get you started:

The LORD (YHVH) is a **shield** around you and the lifter of your head (Psa. 3:3).

_____

_____

_____

The LORD surrounds the righteous person with favor as a **shield** (Psa. 5:12).

_____

_____

_____

The LORD is a **shield** to all who take refuge in Him (Psa. 18:30).

_____

_____

_____

Above all, take up the **shield** of faith to extinguish the flaming arrows (Eph. 6:16).

_____

_____

_____

3. Have you ever been in a worldly fiery furnace? If so, when and why?

_____

_____

_____

4. Do you choose to go through refining processes or do you avoid them by throwing others into the scorching fire?

_____

_____

_____

5. What Babylonian kings have you defeated (or are in the process of defeating) from within? Recall the names of the Babylonian kings reveal the need to overcome darkness, deception, savagery, mercilessness, false positions, and producing after the Tree of Knowledge of Good and Evil.

_____

_____

_____

6. How can the SAMECH (ס) shield of the Lord cause you to sleep better (Song of Solomon 3:7)?

_____

_____

_____

7. God called David a man after his own heart (1 Sam. 13:14). King David learned the hard way that his strength came from the Lord. Investigate what David wrote about ALEF-TAV's SAMECH (ס) "strength."

"I will love You, O LORD, my **strength**. ² The LORD is my rock and my fortress and my deliverer; My God, my **strength**, in whom I will trust; My shield and the horn of my salvation, my stronghold" (Psa. 18:1-2).

_____

_____

_____

"Let the words of my mouth and the meditation of my heart Be acceptable in Your sight, O LORD, my **strength** and my Redeemer" (Psa. 19:14).

_____

_____

_____

"May the LORD answer you in the day of trouble; May the name of the God of Jacob defend you; ² May He send you help from the sanctuary, And **strength**en you out of Zion" (Psa. 20:1-2).

_____

_____

_____

"But You, O LORD, do not be far from Me; O My **Strength**, *hasten to help Me!"* (Psa. 22:19).

_____

_____

_____

"The LORD is my light and my salvation; Whom shall I fear? The LORD is the **strength** *of my life, Of whom shall I be afraid?"* (Psa. 27:1).

_____

_____

_____

"Wait on the LORD; Be of good courage, And He shall **strength**en *your heart; Wait, I say, on the LORD!"* (Psa. 27:14).

_____

_____

_____

"The LORD will give **strength** *to His people; The LORD will bless His people with peace"* (Psa. 29:11).

_____

_____

_____

"For my life is spent with grief, And my years with sighing; My **strength** *fails because of my iniquity, And my bones waste away"* (Psa. 31:10).

_____

_____

_____

"Be of good courage, And He shall **strength**en *your heart, All you who hope in the LORD"* (Psa. 31:24).

_____

_____

_____

SAMECH (ס)

Meditate upon the ALEF-TAV (את) treasures of wisdom that you have learned about SAMECH (ס), which represents support, strength, and shield. What characteristic is most meaningful to you and why?

PRACTICE WRITING SAMECH

● Pronounced *sah-mekh* ●
Start at the top left. Draw an oblong circle.

ס

is dwelling in the harvest hut
of the SUKKAH (סֻכָּה), which
reminds us of God's supreme and
supernatural shelter in the
Wilderness of Sinai (סיני).
Only the One who gave you life
can keep it. Lean into the
peace that the shelter of
SAMECH (ס) brings.

AYIN

WISDOM EIGHTEEN

ע
AYIN

AYIN (ע)

AYIN (ע) is the sixteenth *Hebrew Living™ Letter* of the Alef-Bet whose pronunciation is *ah-yeen*. AYIN (ע) has an ordinal value of 16 and a numerical value of 70, which means that the Hebrews can use it for either the number 16 or 70.

The ancient pictograph for AYIN (ע) agrees with the meaning of its name. In ancient Hebrew AYIN means an eye. The pictograph of an eye for AYIN (ע) symbolizes seeing, understanding, experiencing, and being seen. [40]

AYIN (ע) IN ALEF-TAV (את)

You and I can personally choose to engage the essence of Messiah Yeshua—the Word of God—contained within the Hebrew letter AYIN (ע). The ALEF-TAV (את) redemption for AYIN (ע) focuses on the eyes of the Lord:

> *"The eyes of the Lord are in every place, beholding the evil and the good" (Proverbs 15:3).*

The ways of man are before the eyes of ALEF-TAV (את):

> *"For the ways of man are before the <u>eyes of the Lord</u>, And He ponders all his paths. His own iniquities entrap the wicked man, And he is caught in the cords of his sin" (Proverbs 5:21-22).*

The eyes of ALEF-TAV (את) are throughout the whole earth:

> *"The <u>eyes of the Lord</u> run to and fro throughout the whole earth, to show Himself strong on the behalf of them whose heart is perfect toward Him" (1 Chronicles 16:9).*

ALEF-TAV (את)'s eyes are upon the righteous:

> *"The <u>eyes of the Lord</u> are upon the righteous, and His ears are open unto their cry" (Psalms 34:15).*

---

[40] *Hebrew Word Pictures* by Frank T. Seekins, Ayin, p. 72

ALEF-TAV (את)'s eyes test the righteous because He is righteous:

> *"The Lord is in His holy temple, The Lord's throne is in heaven; <u>His eyes behold</u>, His eyelids test the sons of men. ⁵ The Lord tests the righteous, But the wicked and the one who loves violence His soul hates. ⁶ Upon the wicked He will rain coals; Fire and brimstone and a burning wind shall be the portion of their cup. ⁷ For the Lord is righteous, He loves righteousness; His countenance beholds the upright" (Psalms 11:4-7).*

Notice how the eyes of the LORD preserve knowledge:

> *" ⁹ He who has a <u>generous eye</u> will be blessed, For he gives of his bread to the poor. ¹⁰ Cast out the scoffer, and contention will leave; Yes, strife and reproach will cease. ¹¹ He who loves purity of heart and has grace on his lips, the king will be his friend. ¹² The <u>eyes of the Lord</u> preserve knowledge, But He overthrows the words of the faithless" (Proverbs 22:9-12).*

Knowledge is just one of the Seven Spirits of God, which Scripture connects to the eyes of the Lamb slain before the foundation of the world.

> *" ¹ And I saw in the right hand of Him who sat on the throne a scroll written inside and on the back, sealed with seven seals. ² Then I saw a strong angel proclaiming with a loud voice, 'Who is worthy to open the scroll and to loose its seals?' ³ And no one in heaven or on the earth or under the earth was able to open the scroll, or to look at it. ⁴ So I wept much, because no one was found worthy to open and read the scroll, or to look at it. ⁵ But one of the elders said to me, 'Do not weep. Behold, the Lion of the Tribe of Judah, the Root of David, has prevailed to open the scroll and to loose its seven seals.' ⁶ And I looked, and behold, in the midst of the throne and of the four living creatures, and in the midst of the elders, <u>stood a Lamb as though it had been slain, having</u> seven horns and <u>seven eyes, which are the seven Spirits of God sent out into all the earth</u>" (Revelation 5:1-6).*

Thoughts

The Lamb of God who takes away the sins of the world has many Messianic titles including the Stone of Israel. Notice seven eyes upon the stone before Joshua coincides with the Seven Spirits of God of the Lamb. Always remember that Joshua did not depart from the Tabernacle after Moses spoke to the LORD face to face and returned to the Camp (Exodus 33:11).

" [1] Then he showed me Joshua the high priest standing before the Angel of the Lord, and Satan standing at his right hand to oppose him. [2] And the Lord said to Satan, 'The Lord rebuke you, Satan! The Lord who has chosen Jerusalem rebuke you! Is this not a brand plucked from the fire?' [3] Now Joshua was clothed with filthy garments, and was standing before the Angel. [4] Then He answered and spoke to those who stood before Him, saying, 'Take away the filthy garments from him.' And to him He said, 'See, I have removed your iniquity from you, and I will clothe you with rich robes.' [5] And I said, 'Let them put a clean turban on his head.' So they put a clean turban on his head, and they put the clothes on him. And the Angel of the Lord stood by. [6] Then the Angel of the Lord admonished Joshua, saying, [7] 'Thus says the Lord of hosts: "If you will walk in My ways, And if you will keep My command, Then you shall also judge My house, And likewise have charge of My courts; I will give you places to walk among these who stand here. [8] Hear, O Joshua, the high priest, You and your companions who sit before you, For they are a wondrous sign; For behold, I am bringing forth My Servant the <u>Branch</u>. [9] For behold, the <u>stone</u> that I have laid before Joshua: <u>Upon the stone are seven eyes</u>. Behold, I will engrave its inscription,' Says the Lord of hosts, 'And I will remove the iniquity of that land in one day" (Zechariah 3:1-9).

Another Messianic title for the Lamb having seven eyes (i.e., the Seven Spirits of God) is The Branch.

"There shall come forth a Rod from the stem of Jesse, And a <u>Branch</u> shall grow out of his roots. The Spirit of the Lord shall rest upon Him, The Spirit of wisdom and [the Spirit of] understanding, The Spirit of counsel and [the Spirit of] might, The Spirit of knowledge and [the Spirit of] of the fear of the Lord" (Isaiah 11:1-2 Additions in bracket mine).

Thoughts

The Golden Lampstand (Temple Menorah) is a picture of ALEF-TAV (את) as *"I am the Light of the World" (John 8:12),* which includes the total light spectrum of the Seven Spirits of God.

> *"¹ Now the angel who talked with me came back and wakened me, as a man who is wakened out of his sleep. ² And he said to me, 'What do you see?' So I said, 'I am looking, and there is a <u>lampstand of solid gold</u> with a bowl on top of it, and on the stand seven lamps with seven pipes to the <u>seven lamps</u>. ³ Two olive trees are by it, one at the right of the bowl and the other at its left.' ⁴ So I answered and spoke to the angel who talked with me, saying, 'What are these, my lord?' ⁵ Then the angel who talked with me answered and said to me, 'Do you not know what these are?' And I said, 'No, my lord.' ⁶ So he answered and said to me: 'This is the word of the Lord to Zerubbabel: "Not by might nor by power, but by My Spirit," Says the Lord of hosts. ⁷ 'Who are you, O great mountain? Before Zerubbabel you shall become a plain! And he shall bring forth the capstone with shouts of 'Grace, grace to it!' " ' ⁸ Moreover the word of the Lord came to me, saying: ⁹ 'The hands of Zerubbabel have laid the foundation of this temple; His hands shall also finish it. Then you will know That the Lord of hosts has sent Me to you. ¹⁰ For who has despised the day of small things? For <u>these seven</u> rejoice to see the plumb line in the hand of Zerubbabel. <u>They are the eyes of the Lord, which scan to and fro throughout the whole earth</u>'" (Zechariah 4:1-10).*

> *"And from the throne proceeded lightnings, thunderings, and voices. Seven lamps of fire were burning before the throne, which are the seven Spirits of God" (Revelation 4:5).*

AYIN (ע) represents the spiritual light mentioned in Genesis 1:3, which is different than the celestial light mentioned in Genesis 1:14-18. The divine light of God is greater than the light that emanates from the sun and stars, and its radiance can only be seen with one's inner eye given by the Holy Spirit.

The AYIN (ע) is the Hebrew letter of perception and insight, for its name (עַיִן) means eye. Therefore, from the name of this letter, we understand it encompasses the world of sight both physical and spiritual. "Man's outlook and perception—represented by AYIN—is considered the barometer of his character." [41]

The connection of AYIN with spiritual awareness is first found when Adam and Eve became aware of their sin. *"Then the eyes of both of them were opened, and they realized that they were naked" (Genesis 3:7).* [42] Adam and Eve received new insight. *Targum Yonasan* translates "the eyes of both were enlightened" with an awareness of shame. [43] "Having eaten from the forbidden Tree of Knowledge their bodies came into conflict with their spirit. No longer could they master their senses." [44] The Hebrew Sage "Sforno explains that after the fall of man, their eyes no longer aspired only to the spiritual, but became agents of pleasure and temptations of the flesh." [45] "The eyes see, the heart desires and the person acts. By following his eyes and heart rather than God's will, man lost paradise" (R'Hirsch, Numbers 15:41). [46]

---

[41] *The Wisdom of the Hebrew Alphabet* by Rabbi Michael L. Munk, p. 159
[42] *The Wisdom of the Hebrew Alphabet* by Rabbi Michael L. Munk, p. 172
[43] *The Wisdom of the Hebrew Alphabet* by Rabbi Michael L. Munk, p. 172-173
[44] *The Wisdom of the Hebrew Alphabet* by Rabbi Michael L. Munk, p. 173
[45] *The Wisdom of the Hebrew Alphabet* by Rabbi Michael L. Munk, p. 173
[46] *The Wisdom of the Hebrew Alphabet* by Rabbi Michael L. Munk, p. 173

The Way Of Wisdom

1. When you put Zechariah 4:1-10 together with Revelation 4:5, you can see that the seven lamps before the throne, which are the Seven Spirits of God, are also portrayed as eyes. What are your thoughts about this and other references to the Seven Spirits of God?

Isaiah 11:1-2. _____

_____

Zechariah 3:1-9. _____

_____

Zechariah 4:1-10. _____

_____

Revelation 4:5. _____

_____

Revelation 5:1-6. _____

_____

2. What is most meaningful to you about the "eyes of the Lord"?

_____

_____

3. Pray about and meditate upon the AYIN (ע) eyes of ALEF-TAV (את) represents spiritual light (Gen. 1:3), which is different than the celestial light of Genesis 1:14-18. Write down your flow.

_____

_____

4. What hope do you derive from knowing the "eyes of the Lord" are even on the least of the least?

_____

_____

5. Investigate having the AYIN (ע) eye of your understanding enlightened (Eph. 1:18) by searching out verses that include keys to "understanding" in the Book of Proverbs. This is not an all-inclusive list so feel free to mine more "understanding" riches.

*"A wise man will hear and increase learning, And a man of **understanding** will acquire wise counsel"* *(Prov. 1:5 NASB).*

_____

_____

_____

*"Make your ear attentive to wisdom, Incline your heart to **understanding**" (Prov. 2:2 $_{NASB}$).*

_____
_____
_____

*"For the LORD gives wisdom; From His mouth come knowledge and **understanding**" (Prov. 2:6 $_{NASB}$).*

_____
_____
_____

*"Trust in the LORD with all your heart, And do not lean on your own **understanding**. In all your ways acknowledge Him and He will make your paths straight" (Prov. 3:5-6 $_{NASB}$).*

_____
_____
_____

*"How blessed is the man who finds wisdom, and the man who gains **understanding**. For its profit is better than the profit of silver, and its gain than gold" (Prov. 3:13-14 $_{NASB}$).*

_____
_____
_____

*"Say to wisdom, 'You are my sister,' And call **understanding** your intimate friend" (Prov. 7:4 $_{NASB}$).*

_____
_____
_____

*"Does not wisdom call, And **understanding** lift up her voice? On top of the heights beside the way, Where the paths meet, she takes her stand" (Prov. 8:1-2 $_{NASB}$).*

_____
_____
_____

*" 'Whoever is naïve, let him turn in here!' To him who lacks **understanding** she says, 'Come, eat of my food, And drink of the wine I have mixed. Forsake your folly and live, and proceed in the way of **understanding**' " (Prov. 9:4-6 $_{NASB}$).*

_____
_____
_____

*"The fear of the LORD is the beginning of wisdom, and the knowledge of the Holy One is **understanding**"* (Prov. 9:10 ~NASB~).

_____

_____

_____

*"Good **understanding** produces favor, but the way of the treacherous is hard"* (Prov. 13:15 ~NASB~).

_____

_____

*"A scoffer seeks wisdom, and finds none, but knowledge is easy to him who has **understanding**"* (Prov. 14:6 ~NASB~).

_____

_____

*"He who is slow to anger has great **understanding**, but he who is quick-tempered exalts folly"* (Prov. 14:29 ~NASB~).

_____

_____

*"He who neglects discipline despises himself, but he who listens to reproof acquires **understanding**"* (Prov. 15:32).

_____

_____

*"The wise in heart will be called discerning, and sweetness of speech increases persuasiveness. **Understanding** is a fountain of life to him who has it"* (Prov. 16:21-22a ~NASB~).

_____

_____

_____

*"By wisdom a house is built, and by **understanding** it is established"* (Prov. 24:3 ~NASB~).

_____

_____

_____

AYIN (עַ)

Behold the various gems of wisdom that you have acquired about AYIN (עַ),
which represents the eyes of ALEF-TAV (את). Discern what facet shines most brilliant for you.

PRACTICE WRITING AYIN

♦ The letter AYIN (ע) is pronounced *ah-yeen*. It's a silent letter ♦
Start at the top right to draw a curved line down to the left.
Then start at the top left to draw a straight line to the middle of the curved line.

עַ

is an eye—AYIN (עַיִן)—that sees but doesn't speak. עַ reveals the wondrous and silent humility—ANAVAH (עֲנָוָה)—of serving the Creator. To AVODAH (עֲבוֹדָה) is to work, to worship, and to serve. God's original design in Genesis 2:15 illustrates that our work and our worship are a seamless way of living.

PEY

WISDOM NINETEEN

פ
PEY

PEY/PAY/PE (פ)

PEY (פ) is the seventeenth *Hebrew Living™ Letter* of the Alef-Bet whose pronunciation is *pay*. PEY (פ) has the ordinal value of 17 and a numerical value of 80, which means that the Hebrews can use it for either the number 17 or 80.

The ancient pictograph for PEY (פ) agrees with the meaning of its name. In ancient Hebrew PEY means a mouth. The pictograph of a mouth for PEY (פ) symbolizes speaking, opening, and the beginning (like a river). [47]

PEY (פ) IN ALEF-TAV (את)

You and I can personally choose to engage the essence of Messiah Yeshua—the Word of God—contained within the Hebrew letter PEY (פ). The ALEF-TAV (את) redemption for PEY (פ) focuses on the mouth of the Lord:

> *"So He humbled you, allowed you to hunger, and fed you with manna which you did not know nor did your fathers know, that He might make you know that man shall not live by bread alone; but man lives by every word that proceeds from the <u>mouth of the Lord</u>"* *(Deuteronomy 8:3).*

Notice how the Scriptures that contain the phrase *"the mouth of the LORD"* are extremely encouraging.

> *" 'Come now, and let us reason together,' Says the Lord, 'Though your sins are like scarlet, They shall be as white as snow; Though they are red like crimson, They shall be as wool. [19] If you are willing and obedient, You shall eat the good of the land; [20] But if you refuse and rebel, You shall be devoured by the sword', For the <u>mouth of the Lord</u> has spoken"* *(Isaiah 1:18-20).*

The mouth of the LORD speaks about whatever is true, lovely, a good report, praiseworthy, etc. (Philippians 4:8).

---

[47] *Hebrew Word Pictures* by Frank T. Seekins, Pey, p. 76

" 'Comfort, yes, comfort My people!' Says your God. ² 'Speak comfort to Jerusalem, and cry out to her, That her warfare is ended, That her iniquity is pardoned; For she has received from the Lord's hand Double for all her sins.' ³ The voice of one crying in the wilderness: 'Prepare the way of the Lord; Make straight in the desert A highway for our God. ⁴ Every valley shall be exalted And every mountain and hill brought low; The crooked places shall be made straight And the rough places smooth; ⁵ The glory of the Lord shall be revealed, And all flesh shall see it together; For the <u>mouth of the Lord</u> has spoken' " (Isaiah 40:1-5).

The mouth of the LORD speaks of the delight of the Sabbath.

"If you turn away your foot from the Sabbath, From doing your pleasure on My holy day, And call the Sabbath a delight, The holy day of the Lord honorable, And shall honor Him, not doing your own ways, Nor finding your own pleasure, Nor speaking your own words, ¹⁴ Then you shall delight yourself in the Lord; And I will cause you to ride on the high hills of the earth, And feed you with the heritage of Jacob your father. The <u>mouth of the Lord</u> has spoken" (Isaiah 58:13-14).

The mouth of the LORD speaks of the righteousness and glory of Zion.

"For Zion's sake I will not hold My peace, And for Jerusalem's sake I will not rest, Until her righteousness goes forth as brightness, And her salvation as a lamp that burns. ² The Gentiles shall see your righteousness, And all kings your glory. You shall be called by a new name, Which the <u>mouth of the Lord</u> will name. ³ You shall also be a crown of glory In the hand of the Lord, And a royal diadem In the hand of your God. ⁴ You shall no longer be termed Forsaken, Nor shall your land any more be termed Desolate; But you shall be called Hephzibah [My Delight is In Her], and your land Beulah [Married]; For the Lord delights in you, And your land shall be married. ⁵ For as a young man marries a virgin, So shall your sons marry you; And as the bridegroom rejoices over the bride, So shall your God rejoice over you" (Isaiah 62:1-5 ₐₘₚ Additions in brackets mine).

The mouth of the LORD speaks of the establishment of the mountain of the LORD's House in the latter days.

" ¹ Now it shall come to pass in the latter days That the mountain of the Lord's house shall be established on the top of the mountains, And shall be exalted above the hills; And peoples shall flow to it. ² Many nations shall come and say, 'Come, and let us go up to the mountain of the Lord, To the house of the God of Jacob; He will teach us His ways, And we shall walk in His paths.' For out of Zion the law shall go forth, And the word of the Lord from Jerusalem. ³ He shall judge between many peoples, And rebuke strong nations afar off; They shall beat their swords into plowshares, And their spears into pruning hooks; Nation shall not lift up sword against nation, Neither shall they learn war anymore. ⁴ But everyone shall sit under his vine and under his fig tree, And no one shall make them afraid; For the <u>mouth of the Lord of hosts</u> has spoken. ⁵ For all people walk each in the name of his god, But we will walk in the name of the Lord our God Forever and ever" (Micah 4:1-5).

PEY (פ) encompasses the terms "word," "expression," "speech," "decree," "declaration," etc. In the Hebrew Alphabet, PEY (פ) follows AYIN (ע), which suggests there's a priority of seeing and understanding before the verbal expression of any insight.

The first mention of "mouth" in Scripture is in Genesis 4:11 where it tells us that the earth has a mouth.

"And He said, 'What have you done? The voice of your brother's blood cries out to Me from the ground. ¹¹ So now you are cursed from the earth, which has opened its mouth to receive your brother's blood from your hand'" (Genesis 4:10-11).

Add to this that God defended Moses by saying that He spoke with Moses mouth to mouth.

"¹ Now Miriam and Aaron spoke against Moses because of the Cushite woman whom he had married (for he had married a Cushite woman); ² and they said, 'Has the Lord really spoken only through Moses? Has He not spoken also through us?' And the Lord heard it. ³ (Now the man Moses was very humble (gentle, kind, devoid of self-righteousness), more than any man who was on the face of the earth.) ⁴ Suddenly the Lord said to Moses, Aaron, and Miriam, 'Come out, you three, to the Tent of Meeting (tabernacle).' And the three of them came out. ⁵ The Lord came down in a pillar of cloud and stood at the doorway of the Tabernacle, and He called Aaron and Miriam, and they came forward. ⁶ And He said, 'Hear now My words: If there is a prophet among you, I the Lord will make Myself known to him in a vision And I will speak to him in a dream. ⁷ But it is not so with My servant Moses; He is entrusted and faithful in all My house. ⁸ With him I speak mouth to mouth [directly], Clearly and openly and not in riddles; And he beholds the form of the Lord. Why then were you not afraid to speak against My servant Moses?'" (Numbers 12:1-8ₐₘₚ).

PEY (פ) stands for the mouth, the organ of speech. From the overflow of one's heart, a person speaks.

"⁴⁵ The [intrinsically] good man produces what is good and honorable and moral out of the good treasure [stored] in his heart; and the [intrinsically] evil man produces what is wicked and depraved out of the evil [in his heart]; for his mouth speaks from the overflow of his heart. ⁴⁶ 'Why do you call Me, "Lord, Lord," and do not practice what I tell you? ⁴⁷ Everyone who comes to Me and listens to My words and obeys them, I will show you whom he is like: ⁴⁸ he is like a [far-sighted, practical, and sensible] man building a house, who dug deep and laid a foundation on the rock; and when a flood occurred, the torrent burst against that house and yet could not shake it, because it had been securely built and founded on the rock. ⁴⁹ But the one who has [merely] heard and has not practiced [what I say], is like a [foolish] man who built a house on the ground without any foundation, and the torrent burst against it; and it immediately collapsed, and the ruin of that house was great'" (Luke 6:45-49ₐₘₚ).

King David's heart overflowed with the goodness of the Lord.

> "*My heart is overflowing with a good theme*; I recite my composition concerning the King; My tongue is the pen of a ready writer. ² You are fairer than the sons of men; Grace is poured upon Your lips; Therefore God has blessed You forever" (Psalms 45:1-2). Wisdom, justice, and truth flowed from within David's heart outward through the words of his mouth. " ²⁷ Depart from evil and do good; And you will dwell [securely in the land] forever. ²⁸ For the Lord delights in justice And does not abandon His saints (faithful ones); They are preserved forever, But the descendants of the wicked will [in time] be cut off. ²⁹ The righteous will inherit the land And live in it forever. ³⁰ *The mouth of the righteous proclaims wisdom, And his tongue speaks justice and truth*. ³¹ *The law of his God is in his heart; Not one of his steps will slip*" (Psalms 37:27-31 ₐₘₚ).

The mouth of the righteous flows with joy and wisdom while the wicked speak of perverse things and come to nothing.

> " ²⁸ The hope of the righteous [those of honorable character and integrity] is joy, But the expectation of the wicked [those who oppose God and ignore His wisdom] comes to nothing. ²⁹ The way of the Lord is a stronghold to the upright But it is ruin to those who do evil. ³⁰ The [consistently] righteous will never be shaken, But the wicked will not inhabit the earth.³¹ *The mouth of the righteous flows with [skillful and godly] wisdom*, But the perverted tongue will be cut out.³² The lips of the righteous know (speak) what is acceptable, But *the mouth of the wicked knows (speaks) what is perverted (twisted)*" (Proverbs 10:28-32 ₐₘₚ).

The wise enjoy the good fruit of their month. They reap the abundant life that they sow.

> "A wise son heeds and accepts [and is the result of] his father's discipline and instruction, But a scoffer does not listen to reprimand and does not learn from his errors. ² From *the fruit of his mouth* a [wise] man enjoys good, But the desire of the treacherous is for violence. ³ *The one who guards his mouth [thinking before he speaks] protects his life*; The one who opens his lips wide [and chatters without thinking] comes to ruin" (Proverbs 13:1-3 ₐₘₚ).

Thoughts

The Way Of Wisdom

1. What aspect of "the mouth of the Lord" is most appealing to you?

_____

_____

_____

2. What good words overflow from your heart?

_____

_____

_____

3. What does the Book of Psalms have to say about the "mouth"?

_____

_____

_____

Psalms 5:9. _____

_____

Psalms 10:7. _____

_____

Psalms 17:3. _____

_____

Psalms 18:8. _____

_____

Psalms 19:14. _____

_____

Psalms 33:6. _____

_____

Psalms 37:30. _____

_____

4. What does the Book of Proverbs have to say about the "mouth"?

_____

_____

_____

Proverbs 2:6. _____

_____

Proverbs 4:24. _____

_____

Proverbs 6:2. _____

_____

Proverbs 8:13. _____

_____

Proverbs 10:11. _____

_____

Proverbs 12:14. _____

_____

Proverbs 21:23. _____

_____

5. The pictograph of a mouth for PEY (פ) symbolizes speaking, opening, and the beginning (like a river). What can you learn about "speaking" in the Bible? (Include the words "speak," "spoke" and "spoken".)

"My lips will not **speak** wickedness, Nor my tongue utter deceit" (Job 27:4).

_____

_____

_____

"You shall destroy those who **speak** falsehood; The LORD abhors the bloodthirsty and deceitful man" (Psa. 5:6).

_____

_____

_____

"He who walks uprightly, And works righteousness, And **speaks** the truth in his heart" (Psa. 15:2).

_____

_____

*"My mouth shall **speak** wisdom, And the meditation of my heart shall give understanding" (Psa. 49:3).*

_____
_____
_____

*"For the sin of their mouth and the words of their lips, Let them even be taken in their pride, And for the cursing and lying which they **speak**" (Psa. 59:12).*

_____
_____
_____

*"A true witness delivers souls, But a deceitful witness **speaks** lies" (Prov. 14:25).*

_____
_____
_____

*"Righteous lips are the delight of kings, And they love him who **speaks** what is right" (Prov. 16:13).*

_____
_____
_____

*"A time to tear, And a time to sew; A time to keep silence, And a time to **speak**" (Eccl. 3:7).*

_____
_____
_____

*"They are of the world. Therefore they **speak** as of the world, and the world hears them" (1 John 4:5).*

_____
_____
_____

6. What aspects of ALEF-TAV's emanation of PEY can you learn about "opening"? (Include the words "open" and "opened".)

_____
_____
_____

PEY (פ)

What ALEF-TAV (את) wisdom facet of PEY (פ)'s mouth speaks to you the most?

PRACTICE WRITING PEY

♦ The letter PEY (פ) is pronounced *pay*. ♦

Start on the left at the bottom right of the tongue that hangs down. In one continuous motion draw
a short line to the left go up to the top line and continue around making a backwards capital "C".

① פ →

is the mouth that first speaks
the simple, plain sense truth
—P'SHAT (פשט). However,
everything conceals a myriad of
layers, for everything is a
miracle—PELE (פֶּלֶא). There is an
orchard—PAR'DES (פַּרְדֵּס)—
that belongs to the righteous
whose fruit—P'RIY (פְּרִי)—is the
wisdom of all which is hidden.

WISDOM TWENTY

TSADIK

TSADIK/TZADI/TSADE (צ)

TSADIK (צ) is the eighteenth *Hebrew Living™ Letter* of the Alef-Bet whose pronunciation is *tsah-dee* or *tsah-dek*. TSADIK (צ) has an ordinal value of 18 and a numerical value of 90, which means that the Hebrews can use it for either the number 18 or 90.

In the beginning, this Hebrew letter was called TSADE, which in ancient Hebrew means a fish hook. Today, it is called TSADIK (צ), which means a righteous man. The pictograph for TSADIK (צ) symbolizes to pull forward, something inescapable, desire, trouble, and a harvest. [48]

TSADIK (צ) IN ALEF-TAV (את)

You and I can personally choose to engage the essence of Messiah Yeshua—the Word of God—contained within the Hebrew letter TSADIK (צ). The ALEF-TAV (את) redemption for TSADIK (צ) focuses on righteousness:

> "*16 For I am not ashamed of the <u>gospel of Christ</u>, for it is the power of God to salvation for everyone who believes, for the Jew first and also for the Greek. 17 <u>For in it the righteousness of God</u> is revealed from faith to faith; as it is written, 'The just shall live by faith' "* (Romans 1:16-17).

The precious blood of ALEF-TAV (את) demonstrates the righteousness of God because the price He paid on the Cross allows God's forbearance to pass over our sins when we confess and repent. This is the righteousness of God apart from the law that fulfills the law to all who believe (Matt. 5:17). He is the just and the justifier of the one who has faith in Messiah Yeshua.

> "*21 But now the <u>righteousness of God</u> apart from the law is revealed, being witnessed by the Law and the Prophets, 22 even the <u>righteousness of God</u>, through faith in Jesus Christ, to all and on all who believe. For there is no difference; 23 for all have sinned and fall short of the glory of God, 24 being justified freely by His grace through the redemption that is in Christ Jesus, 25 whom God set forth as a propitiation by His blood, through faith, to demonstrate <u>His righteousness</u>, because in His forbearance God had passed over the sins that were previously committed, 26 to demonstrate at the present time <u>His righteousness</u>, that He might be just and the justifier of the one who has faith in Jesus*" (Romans 3:21-26).

---

[48] *Hebrew Word Pictures* by Frank T. Seekins, Tsadik, p. 80

Righteousness is a gift that reigns in life through ALEF-TAV (את).

> " *17 For if by the one man's offense death reigned through the one, much more those who receive abundance of grace and of the <u>gift of righteousness will reign in life through the One, Jesus Christ</u>. 18 Therefore, as through one man's offense judgment came to all men, resulting in condemnation, even so <u>through one Man's righteous act the free gift came to all men, resulting in justification of life</u>. 19 For as by one man's disobedience many were made sinners, so also <u>by one Man's obedience many will be made righteous</u>. 20 Moreover the law entered that the offense might abound. But where sin abounded, grace abounded much more, 21 so that as sin reigned in death, even so <u>grace might reign through Jesus Christ our Lord</u>" (Romans 5:17-21).*

ALEF-TAV (את)'s Kingdom flows in the Spirit of righteousness, peace, and joy.

> "*17 Therefore do not let your good be spoken of as evil; 17 for the kingdom of God is not eating and drinking, but <u>righteousness and peace and joy in the Holy Spirit</u>. 18 For he who serves Christ in these things is acceptable to God and approved by men" (Romans 14:16-18).*

In Messiah Yeshua your flesh doesn't glory in His presence; because He became for us wisdom from God as well as righteousness, sanctification, and redemption.

> " *26 For you see your calling, brethren, that not many wise according to the flesh, not many mighty, not many noble, are called. 27 But God has chosen the foolish things of the world to put to shame the wise, and God has chosen the weak things of the world to put to shame the things which are mighty; 28 and the base things of the world and the things which are despised God has chosen, and the things which are not, to bring to nothing the things that are, 29 that no flesh should glory in His presence. 30 But of Him <u>you are in Christ Jesus, who became for us wisdom from God— and righteousness and sanctification and redemption</u>— 31 that, as it is written, 'He who glories, let him glory in the Lord' " (1 Corinthians 1:26-31).*

Thoughts

232

God processes and refines our character so that we might become the righteousness of God in Christ. *"For He made Him who knew no sin to be sin for us, that <u>we might become the righteousness of God in Him</u>" (2 Corinthians 5:21).* Due to this being a highly misunderstood topic, please allow me to make a few points. The word "become" in *"we might become the righteousness of God in Him."* means to come into existence (no previous existence), to come to be, to undergo a change or development, or to be suitable. [49] Matthew 6:33 tells us to seek first His righteousness while *Matthew 5:5* declares *"Blessed are those who hunger and thirst for righteousness, for they shall be satisfied."* We don't seek something that we already have, nor do we hunger and thirst for it. For much more on this subject, please refer to the *Hitting the Bull's Eye of Righteousness* book in the *Understanding the Order of Melchizedek: Complete Series* compilation volume. [50] You can also check out the *Sapphire Throne Ministries* WordPress blog for various articles about righteousness, like "Have We Already Been Made the Righteousness of God in Christ?" [51] or "Unlock the Kingly & Bridal Mysteries of Righteousness" [52] or "The Bride's Ancient Foundation of Righteousness." [53]

TSADDIK (צ), "the Righteous One, refers to the Almighty, who is called 'The Righteous and Upright One' (Deut. 32:4), devoid of every conceivable injustice. True righteousness can only exist in God and is an integral part of Him." [54] "The term *TZADDIK* is also applied to human beings, who emulate God's righteousness by conducting themselves with integrity, truth, and justice (Tosefos Yom Tov, Berachos 7:3)."[55]

The Divine *Tzaddik* sustains and protects the world. The human *tzaddik* does too. Just as the angels are God's messengers in heaven, so are *tzaddikim* His ambassadors on earth (Ramban). [56]

---

[49] *Merriam-Webster's Collegiate Dictionary (10th Edition),* "Become." p. 101
[50] *Understanding the Order of Melchizedek: Complete Series. Book 4—Hitting the Bull's Eye of Righteousness.* https://www.amazon.com/Understanding-Order-Melchizedek-Robin-Main/dp/0998598240 /
[51] "Have We Already Beed Made the Righteousness of God in Christ?" by Robin Main. https://sapphirethroneministries.wordpress.com/2013/11/27/have-we-already-been-made-the-righteousness-of-god-in-christ/
[52] "Unlock the Kingly & Bridal Mysteries of Righteousness" by Robin Main. https://sapphirethroneministries.wordpress.com/2018/09/17/unlock-the-kingly-bridal-mysteries-of-righteousness-2/
[53] "The Bride's Ancient Foundation of Righteousness" by Robin Main. https://sapphirethroneministries.wordpress.com/2020/12/24/the-brides-ancient-foundation-of-righteousness/
[54] *The Wisdom in the Hebrew Alphabet* by Michael L. Munk, p. 190
[55] *The Wisdom in the Hebrew Alphabet* by Michael L. Munk, p. 190
[56] *The Wisdom in the Hebrew Alphabet* by Michael L. Munk, p. 190

Thoughts

TSADIK, TZADIK, TZADDI, TSADDI, or TSADE (צ) primarily represents *tzaddikim*—righteous ones. TSADI means to hunt. We are not only hunting for fractured people; but also, for our own soul's lost sparks. Redeemed sparks serve to elevate the consciousness of a soul of the Tsadik to higher levels.

The first mention of "righteous" in Scripture is in Genesis 7:1 when God declares Noah righteous.

> *"Then the Lord said to Noah, 'Come into the ark, you and all your household, because I have seen that <u>you are righteous before Me in this generation</u>' " (Genesis 7:1).*

The father of faith—Abraham—is intimately connected to the realities of righteous and righteousness.

> *"⁵ Then He brought him outside and said, 'Look now toward heaven, and count the stars if you are able to number them.' And He said to him, 'So shall your descendants be.' ⁶ And <u>he believed in the Lord, and He accounted it to him for righteousness</u>" (Genesis 15:5-6).*

The possessor of heaven and earth—Abraham—is the quintessential example of a righteous man of faith who contrary to hope, in hope believed.

> *"¹⁶ The promise depends on faith so that it can be experienced as a grace-gift, and now it extends to all the descendants of Abraham. This promise is not only meant for those who obey the law, but also to those who enter into the faith of Abraham, the father of us all. ¹⁷ That's what the Scripture means when it says: 'I have made you the father of many nations.' He is our example and father, for in God's presence he believed that God can raise the dead and call into being things that don't even exist yet. ¹⁸ Against all odds, when it looked hopeless, Abraham believed the promise and expected God to fulfill it. He took God at His word, and as a result he became the father of many nations. God's declaration over him came to pass: 'Your descendants will be so many that they will be impossible to count!' ¹⁹ In spite of being nearly one hundred years old when the promise of having a son was made, his faith was so strong that it could not be undermined by the fact that he and Sarah were incapable of conceiving a child. ²⁰⁻²¹ He never stopped believing God's promise, for he was made strong in his faith to father a child. And because he was mighty in faith and convinced that God had all the power needed to fulfill his promises, Abraham glorified God! ²² So now you see why Abraham's faith was credited to his account as righteousness before God" (Romans 4:16-22 TPT).*

The righteousness of the faith is not according to the law but by grace. Grace's purpose is obedience (Rom. 1:5). However, never forget that faith without works is dead. (James 2:14-26).

Righteousness and justice are not only the way of the LORD, but they are the foundation and habitation of God's Throne.

> *" ¹⁴ <u>Righteousness and justice are the foundation of Your throne;</u> Lovingkindness and truth go before You. ¹⁵ Blessed and happy are the people who know the joyful sound [of the trumpet's blast]! They walk, O Lord, in the light and favor of Your countenance! ¹⁶ In Your name they rejoice all the day, And <u>in Your righteousness they are exalted</u>" (Psalms 89:14-16 AMP).*

Righteousness is probably one of the most undervalued and misunderstood commodities of the Kingdom of God. Think about it. God instructs us to seek first His righteousness (Matthew 6:33). He tells us to hunger and thirst for righteousness, and that we are blessed when we are persecuted for righteousness' sake. This means that the righteous place we dwell "in Christ" gets enhanced through persecution. We can also say that the purpose behind us being persecuted for His Name's sake is to exhibit the character of Christ, which is founded both in righteousness and justice (Psalms 97:2).[57]

---

[57]*Understanding the Order of Melchizedek: Complete Series* by Robin Main, p. 11-13. https://www.amazon.com/Understanding-Order-Melchizedek-Robin-Main/dp/0998598240/

The Way Of Wisdom

1. How are you seeking to become the righteousness of God in Messiah Yeshua?

_____

_____

_____

2. Why is righteousness a gift that reigns in life? Refer to Rom. 5:17-21.

_____

_____

_____

3. Read the "faith without works is dead" passage (James 2:14-26). Note what the Holy Spirit highlights to you.

_____

_____

_____

4. Romans 6 reveals that obedience leads to righteousness and righteousness leads to holiness (Rom. 6:16,19). Ask the Lord where you can be more obedient to Him.

_____

_____

_____

5. Research the Scriptural references for TSADIK (צ) "righteousness."

_____

_____

*"As for me, I will see Your face in **righteousness**; I shall be satisfied when I awake in Your likeness"* (Psa. 17:15).

_____

_____

*"And that you put on the new man which was created according to God, in true **righteousness** and holiness"* (Eph. 4:24).

_____

_____

*"For the fruit of the Spirit is in all goodness, **righteousness**, and truth"* (Eph. 5:9).

_____

_____

_____

*"By faith Noah, being divinely warned of things not yet seen, moved with godly fear, prepared an ark for the saving of his household, by which he condemned the world and became heir of the **righteousness** which is according to faith"* (Heb. 11:7).

_____

_____

_____

*"Now the fruit of **righteousness** is sown in peace by those who make peace"* (James 3:18).

_____

_____

_____

*"Nevertheless we, according to His promise, look for new heavens and a new earth in which **righteousness** dwells"* (2 Pet. 3:13).

_____

_____

_____

*"Little children, let no one deceive you. He who practices **righteousness** is righteous, just as He is righteous"* (1 John. 3:7).

_____

_____

_____

*"Now I saw heaven opened, and behold, a white horse. And He who sat on him was called Faithful and True, and in **righteousness** He judges and makes war"* (Rev. 19:11).

_____

_____

_____

6. Now, research the Scriptural references for the "righteous" TSADIK (צ).

_____

_____

_____

Genesis 7:1. _____

_____

_____

Exodus 23:7-8. _____

_____

_____

Deuteronomy 32:4. _____

_____

_____

Psalms 1:6. _____

_____

_____

Proverbs 10:11,16,20-21,24-25,28,30-32. _____

_____

_____

Proverbs 11:8-10,21,23,28,30-31. _____

_____

_____

Proverbs 12:10. _____

_____

_____

Romans 5:19. _____

_____

_____

Revelation 16:5. _____

_____

_____

Revelation 19:8. _____

_____

_____

TSADIK (צ)

What ALEF-TAV (את) treasure of wisdom about TSADIK (צ)'s righteousness is most marvelous for you?

PRACTICE WRITING TSADIK

♦ The letter TSADIK (צ) is pronounced *tsah-dee* or *tsah-dek*. ♦

Start at the top left by drawing a diagonal line to your right and continue drawing on the bottom a straight line to your left to match the starting point at the top. Then, lift your pen and put it on the top line above the furthest right point on the bottom. Draw an apostrophe-like line that meets the other drawn line in the center.

is righteousness—TZEDEK (צֶדֶק). The righteous and the humble shall inherit the Earth. The righteous deeds of the saints clothes the Bride of the Messiah (Rev. 19:7-8) whose faith is set like flint upon the Rock—TZUR (צוּר)—that is higher than themselves. Their goal is the joy of the whole earth, which is the True North of the holy hill of TZIYON (צִיּוֹן).

WISDOM TWENTY-ONE

ק
KOOF

KOOF/KUF/QOF (ק)

KOOF (ק) is the nineteenth *Hebrew Living™ Letter* of the Alef-Bet whose pronunciation is *kof* with the sound of "q" as in queen. KOOF (ק) has the ordinal value of 19 and a numerical value of 100, which means that the Hebrews can use it for either the number 19 or 100.

KOOF (ק) in ancient Hebrew means the back of the head. The ancient way this letter was drawn agrees with the meaning of the name of this Hebrew letter. The pictograph for KOOF (ק) is the back of a head, which symbolizes what is behind, what is the last, what is final, and what is the least. [58]

KOOF (ק) IN ALEF-TAV (את)

You and I can personally choose to engage the essence of Messiah Yeshua—the Word of God—contained within the Hebrew letter KOOF (ק). The ALEF-TAV (את) redemption for KOOF (ק) focuses on the back of the Messiah's Head, which corresponds to the Holy of Holies in God's Temple.

The occipital bone is a bone that covers the back of your head. This area is called the occiput, or posterior noggin. The occipital bone is the only bone in your head that connects with your cervical spine (neck). [59] Or in other words, the occipital bone is the only part of a person's skeletal structure that connects their head to their body. Thus, we understand KOOF (ק) represents the Head of the Messiah's vital connection to His Body.

The occipital bone surrounds a large opening known as the *foramen magnum*. The foramen magnum allows key nerves and vascular structures passage between the brain and spine. Namely, it is what the spinal cord passes through to enter the skull. The brainstem also passes through this opening. [60]

The foramen magnum also allows two key blood vessels traversing through the cervical spine, called the vertebral arteries, to enter the inner skull and supply blood to the brain. [61]

The main bone of the occiput is trapezoidal in shape and curves into itself like a shallow dish. This occipital bone overlies the occipital lobes of the cerebrum. The occipital lobes of the cerebrum sit at the back of the head and are responsible for visual processing, like perceiving distance and depth, color, object and face recognition, and memory formation. [62]

---

[58] *Hebrew Word Pictures* by Frank T. Seekins, Koof, p. 84
[59] www.spineuniverse.com
[60] www.spineuniverse.com
[61] www.spineuniverse.com
[62] www.spineuniverse.com

Just like the occipital lobe is in the back of the head and is the smallest lobe of the brain, so is the Holy of Holies, which is in the back of God's Temple, its smallest room.

"Sublime humans based in the heavenly realms who are taking on their cherubic nature (returning to their primordial state before The Fall in the Garden) are part of the Voice of One angelic choir. The priests in Yeshua's day understood that those who stand in God's council and learn wisdom have been born in the Holy of Holies. These are the ones that entered the Holy of Holies and stood/stand before the Throne of the Most High and Holy God and were said to become angels (i.e., take on their cherubic in nature)."[63]

The mysterious union of the earthly and heavenly is portrayed in God's Temple as well as the Head of the Messiah connected to His Body. The Outer Court and Inner Court can represent the earthly (material) realm while the Holy of Holies can represent the eternal heavenly realm.

Numbers Rabbah XV.10 records that in the time of the Messiah that the true temple furnishings would be restored: the fire, the Ark of His Presence, the seven-branched golden lamp, the Spirit, and the Cherubim. These are all keys in this Kingdom Day for the appearance of the fullness of the Messiah bodily. These five are key to the manifestation of the Messiah in His fullness in you. *"Christ in you, the hope of glory" (Colossians 1:27).*

One incredible and glorious manifestation of this happened when Yeshua walked among us on Earth. Now today, another quantum spiritual leap is happening whose aim is for the Mature Body of Christ to attach to its Mature Head—Messiah Yeshua. Its goal is the fullness of the One New Man in Christ personified in the heavenly and mysterious Righteous Metatron Messiah Yeshua figure.

"Yeshua was a man on earth and divine in the heavenlies at the same time. That's who I AM is. Your cherubic nature simply is stepping into the reality of who you are (past the constraints of this world). *So God created man in His own image, in the image of God" (Genesis 1.27).* Never forget that you have been made in God's own image. That means that your original pattern is divine. Don't settle for anything less in your journey to be just like ALEF-TAV (את) back to Eden and beyond." 'Manifesting your cherubic nature' or 'taking on your cherubic nature' is about constantly abiding in Him in heaven and earth [multiplicity within us—our body, soul, and spirit in union with the divine nature]." [64]

"We become so able to reflect Him that we become who we truly are supposed to be. We are the reflection formed out of His Spirit, becoming the Son of God on earth [Hebrews 7.3—the *Great Tsadik*]. The *Great Tsadik*—those in the Order of Melchizedek made like unto the Son of God—takes on the divine nature of God. This is where the Hebrews teach that we take on the Thirteen Attributes of God, which are not forced, but a flowing stream of living water (Exo. 34:6-7)." [65]

"According to Exodus 26.31, the Veil was woven from fine linen, plus blue, purple, and scarlet thread (the assumption is wool, the essence of a lamb). It was *hoseb*, i.e., skilled work. Both Philo and Josephus record what was believed about the Veil in the first century—the time of Yeshua. The four colors represented the four elements from which the world was made:

[1] Red, being fire.
[2] Blue, being air.
[3] Purple, being water.
[4] White, being the earth.

---

[63] *School of the Firmament #6—Angelic Songs of the Sabbath* Class by Robin Main
[64] *MEL GEL Study Guide* by Robin Main, p. 6-10. https://www.amazon.com/MEL-Study-Guide-Robin-Main/dp/0578188538/
[65] *MEL GEL Study Guide* by Robin Main, p. 6-10. https://www.amazon.com/MEL-Study-Guide-Robin-Main/dp/0578188538/

The Mishnah says that the Veil was woven by young women. It measured 20x40 cubits (approximately 10-20 meters). The veil was woven from the four elements, which concealed the glory of God. One side represents matter—the stuff that our three-dimensional visible creation is made of—and the other side is eternity."[66]

"The outer vestment of the High Priest was made out of the same fabric as the Veil, which he wore in the Holy Place or Inner Court. By the way, in the Holy of Holies, the High Priest wore the white linen of the angels. The colored vestments (garments) therefore are associated with the High Priest's role in our visible creation. Josephus and Philo reveal that the outer garment represented the created world. A century before the first century of Philo and Josephus, the Book of the Wisdom of Solomon states in chapter 18, verse 24: 'On Aaron's robe the whole world was depicted.' Thus, the High Priest was an angel (i.e., angelic priest) who emerged from the Holy of Holies into visible creation and clothed himself in the stuff of creation." [67]

"Our physical reality of time and space is only on one side of the Veil. The colored vestment associated with the High Priest's role in visible creation is equivalent to the place where we practically walk out the Order of Melchizedek. NOTE: The only difference between the fabric of the Veil and the fabric of the High Priest's Outer Garment was/is the Cherubim figures embroidered on the Veil (Exodus 26.31; Exodus 36.25)." [68]

"The image of the Cherubim was woven both on the Tabernacle's ten curtains (its one wall) as well as on the Veil. In Hebrew, the Veil is known as the *Paroches*, which means life.

Did you know that only three of the four faces of the living creatures of Ezekiel 1 (called Cherubim in Ezekiel 10)—lion, eagle, and ox—were embroidered in the Tabernacle? Where was the man? The Man—the High Priest—had to be transfigured into the image of the Living Creature/ Cherubim with the four faces of God—lion, ox, eagle, and man—to walk through the Veil."[69]

"Those who pass through (beyond) the Veil find themselves outside time—the eternal realm. We are told that when Rabbi Ishmael ascended and looked back, he saw the curtain (Veil) on which was depicted past, present, and future.

> *"All generations to the end of time were printed on the curtain of the Omnipresent One. I saw them all with my own eyes" (3 Enoch 45.6).*

The *Apocalypse of Abraham (21.1)* describes how the patriarch ascended, and then looked down and saw all creation foreshadowed on the firmament. Not only can we think of the Holy Place as the earthly realm ("on earth") and the Holy of Holies as the heavenly eternal realm ("as it is in heaven"), but the Veil can also be thought of as a portal between heaven and earth. There's also an arc between heaven and earth between your two ears." [70]

"When the High Priest functioned in our visible creation, he wore the sacred name YHVH on his forehead, because he represented the Lord of Hosts dwelling with His people. *"Blessed is he who comes with/in the Name of the Lord."*

The Veil and the High Priest's outer garment being made of identical fabric is key to the concept of Incarnation (being begotten)—both Yeshua's Incarnation (who is the Mature Head of the Body of Christ) and His Mature Body (you and me)."[71]

[66]*MEL GEL Study Guide* by Robin Main, p. 6-10. https://www.amazon.com/MEL-Study-Guide-Robin-Main/dp/0578188538/
[67]*MEL GEL Study Guide* by Robin Main, p. 6-10. https://www.amazon.com/MEL-Study-Guide-Robin-Main/dp/0578188538/
[68]*MEL GEL Study Guide* by Robin Main, p. 6-10. https://www.amazon.com/MEL-Study-Guide-Robin-Main/dp/0578188538/
[69]*MEL GEL Study Guide* by Robin Main, p. 6-10. https://www.amazon.com/MEL-Study-Guide-Robin-Main/dp/0578188538/
[70]*MEL GEL Study Guide* by Robin Main, p. 6-10. https://www.amazon.com/MEL-Study-Guide-Robin-Main/dp/0578188538/
[71]*MEL GEL Study Guide* by Robin Main, p. 6-10. https://www.amazon.com/MEL-Study-Guide-Robin-Main/dp/0578188538/

The Way Of Wisdom

1. What is the multidimensional reality of I AM?

_____

_____

_____

2. How does a person raise their level of holiness and sanctity (Rom. 6)?

_____

_____

_____

3. Investigate the "Holy of Holies," which is also called the "Most Holy Place" as well as "The Oracle."

_____

_____

_____

"Holy of Holies" or "Holiest of All" (Heb. 9:8).

_____

_____

_____

"Most Holy Place" (1 Kings 6:16; 7:50; 8:6; 2 Chron. 3:8,10; 4:22; 5:7,11; Ezek. 41:4; Heb. 9:12,25)

_____

_____

_____

"The Oracle" (1 Kings 6:5,16,19,20-23; 1 Kings 8:6 in KJV) _____

_____

_____

_____

4. Research the Scriptural references for KOOF (ק) "holiness."

_____

_____

_____

_____

Exodus 15:11. _____

_____

_____

_____

Exodus 28:36. _____

_____

_____

_____

Psalms 29:2. _____

_____

_____

_____

Psalms 89:35. _____

_____

_____

_____

Psalms 110:3. _____

_____

_____

_____

Isaiah 35:8. _____

_____

_____

_____

Zechariah 14:20-21. _____

_____

_____

_____

Romans 1:4. _____

_____

_____

_____

2 Corinthians 7:1. _____

_____

_____

_____

1 Thessalonians 3:13. _____

_____

_____

_____

5. The pictograph for KOOF (ק) is of the back of the head and it symbolizes what is behind, what is the last, what is final, and what is the least. What aspects of ALEF-TAV's emanation of KOOF (ק) can you learn about "last"? Recommended Scriptures are Matt. 20:16; Mark 15:37; John 6:39-54; John 7:37; John 11:24; 1 Cor. 15:26-52; 2 Tim. 3:1; Heb. 1:2; Jam. 5:3; 2 Pet. 3:3; 1 John 2:18; Rev. 1:11,17; 2:8; 22:13. Please read in context. There are many more verses that contain "last."

_____

_____

_____

_____

_____

_____

_____

_____

_____

6. What aspects of ALEF-TAV's emanation of KOOF (ק) can you learn about "final"? Only one verse in the NKJV—Jeremiah 12:4— has the word "final" in its translation, but other verses carry the concepts of "finally" and "finished."

_____

_____

_____

_____

_____

_____

_____

_____

7. What aspects of ALEF-TAV's emanation of KOOF (ק) can you learn about "least"? Recommended Scriptures are Gen. 32:10; Deut. 7:7; 1 Sam. 9:21; Jer. 31:34; Matt. 2:6; Matt. 11:11; 13:32; 25:40-45; Luke. 9:48; 16:10; Acts 5:15; 1 Cor. 15:9; Eph. 3:8; Heb. 8:11.

_____

_____

_____

_____

_____

_____

_____

_____

_____

KOOF (ק)

What ALEF-TAV (את) gem of wisdom about KOOF (ק)'s holiness is most splendid to you?

PRACTICE WRITING KOOF

♦ The letter KOOF (ק) is pronounced *kof* with the sound of "q" as in queen. ♦
Start at the top left by drawing a swooping arc to your right and down. Then, lift your pen and draw a line
straight down from where you started on the top left, leaving a space between.

ק

is the call of holy—KADOSH
(קָדוֹשׁ). KOOF (ק) is the voice—
KOL (קוֹל)—of a person
proclaiming the oneness and the
glory of God. ק is the infinite
worship before the Throne:
*"Holy, holy, holy, Lord God
Almighty" (Rev. 4:8).*

RESH/REYSH (ר)

RESH (ר) is the twentieth *Hebrew Living™ Letter* of the Alef-Bet whose pronunciation is *raysh*. RESH (ר) has an ordinal value of 20 and a numerical value of 200, which means that the Hebrews can use it for either the number 20 or 200.

RESH (ר) in ancient Hebrew means a head. The ancient way this letter was drawn agrees with the meaning of the name of this Hebrew letter. The pictograph for RESH (ר) symbolizes a person, what is the highest, and what is most important. [72]

RESH (ר) IN ALEF-TAV (את)

You and I can personally choose to engage the essence of Messiah Yeshua—the Word of God—contained within the Hebrew letter RESH (ר). The ALEF-TAV (את) redemption for RESH (ר) focuses on the Messiah being the Head that guides and directs His Body.

"The Order of Melchizedek's goal is to bear the record of the testimony of God's DNA in one's body to be ONE BODY: *"There is one body and one Spirit, just as also you were called in one hope of your calling"* (Ephesians 4:4 *NASB*).

The one body is the Body of the Messiah that's connected to its Head—ALEF-TAV (את). In its fullness is the undifferentiated state of the Messiah. This fully mature Son of Man is portrayed in Revelation 1. By the way, the Lord told me that His angel in Revelation 1:1 is the righteous Metatron.

> *"¹ This is a revelation from Jesus Christ, which God gave him to show his servants the events that must soon take place. He sent an angel to present this revelation to his servant John, ² who faithfully reported everything he saw. This is his report of the word of God and the testimony of Jesus Christ. ³ God blesses the one who reads the words of this prophecy to the church, and he blesses all who listen to its message and obey what it says, for the time is near. ⁴ This letter is from John to the seven churches in the province of Asia. Grace and peace to you from the one who is, who always was, and who is still to come; from the sevenfold Spirit before his throne; ⁵ and from Jesus Christ. He is the faithful witness to these things, the first to rise from the dead, and the ruler of all the kings of the world. All glory to him who loves us*

---

[72] *Hebrew Word Pictures* by Frank T. Seekins, Reysh, p. 88

and has freed us from our sins by shedding his blood for us. ⁶ *He has made us a <u>Kingdom of priests</u> for God His Father. All glory and power to Him forever and ever! Amen.* ⁷ *Look! He comes with the clouds of heaven. And everyone will see him—even those who pierced him. And all the nations of the world will mourn for him. Yes! Amen!* ⁸ *'I am the Alpha and the Omega—the beginning and the end,' says the Lord God. 'I am the one who is, who always was, and who is still to come—the Almighty One.'* ⁹ *I, John, am your brother and your partner in suffering and in God's Kingdom and in the patient endurance to which Jesus calls us. I was exiled to the island of Patmos for preaching the word of God and for my testimony about Jesus.* ¹⁰ *It was the Lord's Day, and I was worshiping in the Spirit. Suddenly, I heard behind me a loud voice like a trumpet blast.* ¹¹ *It said, 'Write in a book everything you see, and send it to the seven churches in the cities of Ephesus, Smyrna, Pergamum, Thyatira, Sardis, Philadelphia, and Laodicea.'* ¹² *When I turned to see who was speaking to me, I saw seven gold lampstands.* ¹³ *And standing in the middle of the lampstands was <u>someone like the Son of Man</u>. He was wearing a long robe with a gold sash across his chest.* ¹⁴ *<u>His head and his hair were white</u> like wool, as white as snow. And his eyes were like flames of fire.* ¹⁵ *His feet were like polished bronze refined in a furnace, and his voice thundered like mighty ocean waves"* (Revelation 1:1-15 _{NLT}).

Notice that the one like the Son of Man has white hair on His head. Throughout Scripture, the Head of the Body of the Messiah is portrayed as Yeshua:

> *"But I want you to know that <u>the head of every man is Christ</u>, the head of woman is man, and the head of Christ is God"* (1 Corinthians 11:3).

> *"* ⁸ *Therefore He says: 'When He ascended on high, He led captivity captive, And gave gifts to men.'* ⁹ *(Now this, 'He ascended'—what does it mean but that He also first descended into the lower parts of the earth?* ¹⁰ *He who descended is also the One who ascended far above all the heavens, that He might fill all things.)* ¹¹ *And He Himself gave some to be apostles, some prophets, some evangelists, and some pastors and teachers,* ¹² *for the equipping of the saints for the work of ministry, for the edifying of the body of Christ,* ¹³ *till we all come to the unity of the faith and of the knowledge of the Son of God, to a perfect man, to the measure of the stature of the fullness of Christ;* ¹⁴ *that we should no longer be children, tossed to and fro and carried about with every wind of doctrine, by the trickery of men, in the cunning craftiness of deceitful plotting,* ¹⁵ *but, speaking the truth in love, <u>may grow up in all things into Him who is the head—Christ—</u>* ¹⁶ *<u>from whom the whole body</u>, joined and knit together by what every joint supplies, according to the effective working by which every part does its share, causes growth of the body for the edifying of itself in love"* (Ephesians 4:8-16).

> *"* ¹⁶ *Therefore no one is to act as your judge in regard to food or drink or in respect to a festival or a new moon or a Sabbath day—* ¹⁷ *things which are a mere shadow of what is to come; but the substance belongs to Christ.* ¹⁸ *Let no one keep defrauding you of your prize by delighting in self-abasement and the worship of the angels, taking his stand on visions he has seen, inflated without cause by his fleshly mind,* ¹⁹ *and <u>not holding fast to the head</u>, from whom the entire body, being supplied and held together by the joints and*

ligaments, grows with a growth which is from God. ²⁰ If you have died with Christ to the elementary principles of the world, why, as if you were living in the world, do you submit yourself to decrees, such as, ²¹ 'Do not handle, do not taste, do not touch it!' ²² (which all refer to things destined to perish with use) –in accordance with the commandments and teachings of men? ²³ These are matters which have, to be sure, the appearance of wisdom in self-made religion and self-abasement and severe treatment of the body, but are of no value against fleshly indulgence" (Colossians 2:16-23 ₙₐₛв).

The fully mature Head of Messiah Yeshua can only fully and properly attach to a Fully Mature Resurrected Body of Believers. The Fully Mature Resurrected Body of Believers are people who embody earnestly and persistently holding fast to the Head and growing up in all aspects into the Messiah.

The culmination of holding fast to the Head to the utmost is what I call the undifferentiated state of the Messiah in which the Messiah's Head and His Body are indistinguishable because they are one. This is the oneness matrix of Messiah Yeshua. I like to call it the Oneness Metatron Matrix; because the white-haired fully mature Head of the Messiah and His fully mature Body is in a word, Metatron; or in other words, the righteous Metatron Messiah.

There is another Metatron that's the false Messiah—Metatron Mithra—that is so close to the real Messiah that a person needs to completely die to themselves and their own desires to see its reality. Currently, many Christians believe that they are connecting to the true Messiah during Christmas, but history and Scripture reveal a different reality. Always remember Yeshua celebrated Hanukkah, not Christmas:

> " ²² *And it was at Jerusalem the Feast of Dedication [Hanukkah] and it was winter. ²³ And Jesus walked in the Temple in Solomon's Porch"* (John 10:22-23 ₖⱼᵥ ₐddition mine).

> " ¹¹ *Unto you has been given to know the mystery of the Kingdom of God: but unto them that are without all these things are done in parables. ¹² For seeing they see, and yet do not perceive; and hearing they hear, and yet do not understand; if they should return, their sin would be forgiven. ¹³ And he said to them, Do you not understand this parable? How then will you understand all the parables?"* (Mark 4:11-13 ₗₐₘₛₐ's ₐᵣₐₘₐᵢc).

The parable that Yeshua is talking about in Mark 4:13 is the Parable of the Sower. Yeshua tells us plainly that the seed is the Word of God, and this seed is sown in our hearts (Luke 8:11; Mark 4:15). Therefore, the Word of God is key to unlocking the various mysteries of God deposited in one's heart.

While doing an extensive study about "mysteries" and "mystery" in Scripture, I happened upon the following definition for "mystery" in my *Merriam-Webster's Collegiate Dictionary (10ᵗʰ Edition)*.

mystery ~ *noun* : a religious truth that one can know only by revelation and cannot fully understand : a Christian sacrament (1) a secret religious rite believed (as in Eleusian and Mithraic Cults) to impart enduring bliss to the initiate (2) a cult devoted to such rites. [73]

Now hold on there. According to the Word of God, a Mithraic cult devoted to sun god worship should not be connected to a true and righteous Christian sacrament; but it was, and still is. Mithra was one of the

---

favorite sun gods adopted by Rome, just before Christmas got institutionalized in the Church. Mithra was the Persian version of the original Babylonian sun god Tammuz. The *Catholic Encyclopedia* itself credits Mithra's Winter Festival, as claiming strong responsibility for the December 25th date for Christmas.

Mithra's Winter Festival was a birth celebration for *Sol Invictus Mithra*, which was also called "The Nativity," "The Nativity of the Sun," or "The Nativity of the Unconquered Sun."

Even though the phrase "Christ's mass" (i.e., Christmas) is first found in 1038 AD, according to the *Catholic Encyclopedia*, I use the term to help everyone track our modern winter revels with those of the past. Prior to the 11th Century, Christmastime was associated with the Winter Solstice, Midwinter, or Winter Revels. For simplicity's sake, I say "Christmas" most times instead of the Winter Solstice. The first recorded evidence of "Christmas" taking place on December 25th isn't found until the time of Constantine in 336 AD. History records that Constantine was a very devout worshipper of the sun god *Sol Invictus Mithra*.

The Emperor not only presided over the Nicene Council but spearheaded building The Vatican atop the hill where the Mithra Cult worshipped the sun. I go into all this in the "Constantine Compromises" section of "Chapter 5—The Golden Snare" in *SANTA-TIZING: What's wrong with Christmas and how to clean it up*. [74]

It has been given to the sons of the Living God to know the Mithraic Cult Mystery. Christmas was originally a secret religious rite for the pagan elite in Rome. The Mithraic Cult was devoted to worshipping the birth day of their sun god on the ancient winter solstice. Throughout antiquity, the celebrated birthday of ALL sun gods was the ancient winter solstice, which was December 25th before the Roman shift in time. The origins of the birthday of the sun god(s) are rooted in Babylon, specifically, Chaldea where sorcery (lies, control, manipulation), sun god worship (Christmas), and the land of merchant status (materialism) originated.

Its original icon was a golden calf said to represent the divinity of the ancient Chaldean god Saturn. Though my dictionary says that the Mithraic Cult had a secret religious rite believed to impart bliss to the initiate, an honest glance reveals that *"This wisdom is not that which comes down from above, but is earthly, natural, demonic" (James 3:15 NASB)*. The roots of Christmas connect its participants to bowing down to the pagan sun gods under a tree, which hinders the most supreme eternal bliss—becoming part of the Bride of the Messiah and part of the Oneness Metatron Matrix—for those who worship at Mithra's Table. Note: This is not about salvation, but eternal rewards.

Recall that Metatron is the undifferentiated state of the Messiah—the Mature Head and the Transfigured/Transformed Cherubic Body of Christ. Believers can be, and are, part of the One New Man in Christ on earth; but Metatron consists of people who have literally become just like Yeshua. These devout souls have been transfigured, or you could say transformed, fully mature cells of the fully Mature Body of Christ attached to the Fully Mature Head—Messiah Yeshua. [75]

It seems strange that the letter RESH (ר) which stands for "head" and "beginning" appears towards the end of the Hebrew Alphabet. It is significant that RESH (ר) is used to symbolize both a "wicked person" (*Rasa'* רשע) and a "leader, chief, head" (*Rosh* ראש). It teaches that a penitent can attain the extraordinary accomplishment of transforming himself completely from the lowest status to the highest. (Midrash Alpha Beis).

[74]*SANTA-TIZING: What's wrong with Christmas and how to clean it up* by Robin Main. https://www.amazon.com/SANTA-TIZING-Whats-wrong-Christmas-clean/dp/1607911159/

[75]*Understanding the Order of Melchizedek: Complete Series* by Robin Main, p. 487-494. https://www.amazon.com/Understanding-Order-Melchizedek-Robin-Main/dp/0998598240/

The Way Of Wisdom

1. Ask the Lord about Christ's mature Head attaching to a mature Body (Rev. 1:14).

_____

_____

_____

_____

2. How can you "hold fast to the Head" (Eph. 4:18; Col. 2:19)?

_____

_____

_____

_____

3. There are 12 biblical titles for Messiah Yeshua, which have to do with RESH (ר) and _rosh_ (head). These scriptures leave no doubt about the supremacy of the Anointed One. [76]

_____

_____

_____

_____

_____

[1] "Chief Cornerstone" (Eph. 2:19-22; 1 Pet. 2:1-10). _____

_____

_____

[2] "Head of the corner" (Psa. 118:15-23). _____

_____

_____

[3] "Head of the Body" (Col. 1:12-20). _____

_____

_____

[4] "Head of the Church" (Eph. 1:21-22; Eph. 5:22-23). _____

_____

_____

_____

[76]_Messiah and His Hebrew Alphabet_ by Dick Mills & David Michael, p. 116-117

[5] "Firstfruits" (Lev. 23:9-14; Rom. 8:23; 1 Cor. 15:20,23; James 1:18; Rev. 14:4).

_____

_____

_____

_____

[6] "Firstborn of the Dead" (Col. 1:18). _____

_____

_____

_____

[7] "Firstbegotten" (Heb. 1:6 KJV). _____

_____

_____

_____

[8] "Firstborn" (Rom. 8:29; Heb. 12:23). _____

_____

_____

_____

[9] "Firstborn Son" (Luke 2:7). _____

_____

_____

_____

[10] "Captain of our Salvation" (Heb. 2:10). _____

_____

_____

_____

[11] "The First" (Isa. 41:4; 44:6; 48:12; Rev. 1:11,17; 2:8; 22:13). _____

_____

_____

_____

[12] "Ruler" (Micah 5:2). _____

_____

_____

_____

4. The undifferentiated state of the Messiah means no difference. It's like the oneness of the Heavenly Father and Messiah Yeshua. If Yeshua gave His all to have a place to lay His Head (Matt. 8:20), would He ask His Bride to do nothing less?

_____

_____

_____

_____

_____

_____

_____

_____

_____

5. What does it mean to be crucified in union with Christ (Gal. 2:20)? What does it mean to know Him, the power of His resurrection, and the fellowship of His suffering by being conformed to His death (Phil. 3:10)?

_____

_____

_____

_____

_____

_____

_____

_____

RESH (ר)

What nugget of the ALEF-TAV (את)'s Head revealed by RESH (ר) stands out to you?

PRACTICE WRITING RESH

♦ The letter RESH (ר) is pronounced *raysh*. ♦

Start at the top left by drawing a line to your right that bends in the upper top right corner
and continues straight down until your pen meets the bottom line.

ר

is ultimately about being closer
to the Head—ROSH (רֹאשׁ)—of
the Body of the Messiah than to
anyone else. We speak the truth
in love, so all things may grow up
and attach correctly to the Head;
thus, we hold fast to the Head
that nourishes and sustains
the Body of Christ.

SHIN

WISDOM TWENTY-THREE

SHIN

SHIN/SHEEN (ש)

SHIN (ש) is the twenty-first *Hebrew Living™ Letter* of the Alef-Bet whose pronunciation is *sheen*. SHIN (ש) has an ordinal value of 21 and a numerical value of 300, which means that the Hebrews can use it for either the number 21 or 300.

SHIN (ש) in ancient Hebrew means a tooth. The ancient way this letter was drawn agrees with the meaning of the name of this Hebrew letter. The pictograph for SHIN (ש) is of teeth, which symbolizes devouring, consuming, destroying, or something sharp. [77]

SHIN (ש) IN ALEF-TAV (את)

You and I can personally choose to engage the essence of Messiah Yeshua—the Word of God—contained within the Hebrew letter SHIN (ש). The ALEF-TAV (את) redemption for SHIN (ש) focuses on the Messiah's connection to the Mountain of God and being El Shaddai.

Sinai's name is derived from the Hebrew word for tooth—*shen*—from which we get the Hebrew letter SHIN (ש). Shen means tooth, sharp, crag, cliff, ivory, and forefront. [78]

Let's look at "sharp" and "craggy." Mountain ranges with sharp, craggy, tooth-like peaks often bear the name "Sierra," like the Sierra Nevada or the Sierra Madre. In Spanish, the word "sierra" literally means "the teeth of a saw" or "sawtooth." From a distance, the outline of distant sharp mountain peaks can look like the teeth of a saw blade. Similarly, Sinai comes from the letter SHIN (ש); and therefore, describes the sharp, craggy, tooth-like rocky and rugged spires of the Sinai mountain range. [79]

Although Sinai is spelled with the letter SAMECH (ס), it is not uncommon for SHIN (ש) to be substituted for SAMECH and vice versa. One of the alternate names for Mount Sinai is *Har Bashan*—"the mountain with the teeth." The Hebrew Sages say that *Har Bashan* suggests that "mankind through the virtue of this mountain obtains its sustenance."[80] Many moons ago the Lord told me that Mount Sinai was Mount Zion on the other side of the Cross. Please refer to Hebrews 12:18-29 and Galatians 4:22-31.

---

[77] *Hebrew Word Pictures* by Frank T. Seekins, Sheen, p. 92
[78] *Messiah and His Hebrew Alphabet* by Dick Mills and David Michael, p. 121
[79] *Messiah and His Hebrew Alphabet* by Dick Mills and David Michael, p. 121
[80] *Messiah and His Hebrew Alphabet* by Dick Mills and David Michael, p. 121

SHIN (ש) is shorthand for *El Shaddai*. The Book of Job has the most references to "Almighty" God—*El Shaddai*—and it's connected to destruction, discipline, and restoration.

[1] " *¹³ This is the portion of a wicked person from God, And the inheritance which tyrants receive from the Almighty: ¹⁴ Though his sons are many, they are destined for the sword; And his descendants will not be satisfied with bread. ¹⁵ His survivors will be buried because of the plague, And their widows will not be able to weep. ¹⁶ Though he piles up silver like dust, And prepares garments as plentiful as the clay, ¹⁷ He may prepare it, but the righteous will wear it And the innocent will divide the silver. ¹⁸ He has built his house like the spider's web, Or a hut which the watchman has made. ¹⁹ He lies down rich, but never again; He opens his eyes, and it no longer exists. ²⁰ Terrors overtake him like a flood; A storm steals him away in the night. ²¹ The east wind carries him away, and he is gone; For it sweeps him away from his place" (Job 27:13-21 ₙₐₛ_B).*

[2] " *¹⁷ Behold, happy is the person whom God disciplines, So do not reject the discipline of the Almighty. ¹⁸ For He inflicts pain, and gives relief; He wounds, but His hands also heal. ¹⁹ In six troubles He will save you; Even in seven, evil will not touch you. ²⁰ In famine He will redeem you from death, And in war, from the power of the sword. ²¹ You will be hidden from the scourge of the tongue, And you will not be afraid of violence when it comes. ²² You will laugh at violence and hunger, And you will not be afraid of wild animals. ²³ For you will be in league with the stones of the field, And the animals of the field will be at peace with you. ²⁴ You will know that your tent is secure, For you will visit your home and have nothing missing" (Job 5:17-24 ₙₐₛ_B).*

[3] " *²¹ Be reconciled with Him, and be at peace; Thereby good will come to you. ²² Please receive instruction from His mouth, And put His words in your heart. ²³ If you return to the Almighty, you will be restored; If you remove injustice far from your tent, ²⁴ And put your gold in the dust, And the gold of Ophir among the stones of the brooks, ²⁵ Then the Almighty will be your gold and abundant silver to you. ²⁶ For then you will take pleasure in the Almighty And lift up your face to God. ²⁷ You will pray to Him, and He will hear you; And you will pay your vows. ²⁸ You will also decide something, and it will be established for you; And light will shine on your ways. ²⁹ When they have brought you low, you will speak with confidence, And He will save the humble person. ³⁰ He will rescue one who is not innocent, And he will be rescued due to the cleanness of your hands" (Job 22:21-30 ₙₐₛ_B).*

Thoughts

The Almighty's great name "Shaddai" literally bears the letter SHIN (ש). The attributes of *El Shaddai* are: Almighty; All Powerful; All Sufficient One; Judge; the sweet omnipotence of love, sure and all-sufficient resource in time of need; power to fulfill every promise; bountiful; overrides nature to perform miracles and remove mountains; giver and pourer out of self-sacrificial love and blessing; nurturer and comforter that gives strength and quiets the restless, and in Him all fullness dwells.

Eternity has been put in your heart:

> *"He has made everything appropriate in its time. He has also <u>set eternity in their heart</u>, without the possibility that mankind will find out the work which God has done from the beginning even to the end" (Ecclesiastes 3:11 NASB).*

SHIN (ש)—*El Shaddai* (the Almighty, Unlimited God)—is also written on your heart. *"19 And I will give them one heart, and put a new spirit within them. And I will remove the heart of stone from their flesh and give them a heart of flesh, 20 so that they may walk in My statutes, and keep My ordinances and do them. Then they will be My people, and I shall be their God" (Ezekiel 11:19-20 NASB).* The lower and larger left ventricle of a human's heart supplies blood to the entire body while the smaller right ventricle (which supplies the lungs) is positioned like the lines of the letter SHIN (ש). Therefore, SHIN (ש)—*El Shaddai*—is written on your heart.

Additionally, God has placed His name literally in Jerusalem. Notice that a topographical map of Jerusalem reveals its mountains form the Hebrew letter SHIN (ש)—*El Shaddai*. God says, *"I have chosen Jerusalem for My Name to be there" (2 Chronicles 6:6).*

The same phenomenon appears in Shiloh where the Tabernacle stood for 369 years. God's Name (ש) is imprinted on the land of Israel.

> *"I have heard the prayer and the plea you have made before Me; I have consecrated this temple which you have built, by putting My Name there forever. My eyes and My heart will always be there" (1 Kings 9:3).*

The Vulcan hand salute of StarTrek's Leonard Nimoy comes from how the priests *(kohens)* form the letter SHIN (ש) with their hands when they recite the priestly blessing.

> *"22 Then the Lord spoke to Moses, saying, 23 'Speak to Aaron and to his sons, saying, "In this way you shall bless the sons of Israel. You are to say to them: 24 The Lord bless you, and keep you; 25 The Lord cause His face to shine on you, And be gracious to you; 26 The Lord lift up His face to you, And give you peace.' 27 So they shall invoke My name on the sons of Israel, and then I will bless them" ' " (Numbers 6:22-27 NASB).*

Thoughts

269

The Way Of Wisdom

1. What attribute(s) of *El Shaddai* stands out most to you and why?

_____

_____

_____

_____

_____

2. Investigate Mount Sinai's connection to Mount Zion (Heb. 12:18-29 and Gal.4:22-31).

_____

_____

_____

_____

3. Research "Mount Zion" more thoroughly in Scripture.

_____

_____

_____

_____

_____

2 Kings 19:31. _____

_____

Psalms 48:2. _____

_____

Psalms 74:2. _____

_____

Psalms 125:1. _____

_____

_____

Joel 2:1. _____

_____

_____

Hebrews 12:22. _____

_____

_____

Revelation 14:4. _____

_____

_____

4. Now add more depth by researching "Zion." Notice how it matches the SHIN (ש) written by the mountains of Jerusalem.

*"Nevertheless David took the stronghold of **Zion** (that is, the City of David)" (2 Sam. 5:7).*

_____

_____

_____

*"Yet I have set My King On My holy hill of **Zion**" (Psa. 2:6).* _____

_____

_____

*"May He send you help from the sanctuary, And strengthen you out of **Zion**" (Psa. 20:2).*

_____

_____

_____

*"Out of **Zion**, the perfection of beauty, God will shine forth" (Psa. 50:2).* _____

_____

_____

*"Do good in Your good pleasure to **Zion**; Build the walls of Jerusalem" (Psa. 51:18).*

_____

_____

_____

*"For the LORD shall build up **Zion**; He shall appear in His glory"* (Psa. 102:16).

_____

_____

_____

_____

*"The LORD shall send the rod of Your strength out of **Zion**. Rule in the midst of Your enemies!"* (Psa. 110:2). _____

_____

_____

_____

*"The LORD bless you out of **Zion**, And may you see the good of Jerusalem All the days of your life"* (Psa. 128:5).

_____

_____

_____

_____

*"For the LORD has chosen **Zion**; He has desired it for His dwelling place"* (Psa. 132:13).

_____

_____

_____

_____

*"The LORD who made heaven and earth Bless you from **Zion**!"* (Psa. 134:3).

_____

_____

_____

_____

*"**Zion** shall be redeemed with justice, And her penitents with righteousness"* (Isa. 1:27).

_____

_____

_____

_____

*"Many people shall come and say, 'Come, and let us go up to the mountain of the LORD, To the house of the God of Jacob; He will teach us His ways, And we shall walk in His paths.' For out of **Zion** shall go forth the law, And the word of the LORD from Jerusalem" (Isa. 2:3).*

_____

_____

_____

_____

5. Why would God write a SHIN (ש) on a person's heart? Consider the attributes of the All-Sufficient, Almighty God *(El Shaddai)* again.

_____

_____

_____

_____

_____

_____

6. Contemplate that you are a letter of Christ written by the Spirit of the Living God on the SHIN (ש) tablets of your heart (2 Cor. 3:2-3).

_____

_____

_____

_____

_____

_____

7. Further investigate the references to "Almighty"—*El Shaddai*—in the Book of Job (Job 8:3; Job 11:7; Job 13:3; etc.). Recall Almighty God is connected to destruction, discipline, and restoration.

_____

_____

_____

_____

_____

_____

SHIN (שׁ)

Meditate upon the ALEF-TAV (את) treasures of wisdom that you have learned about SHIN (שׁ), which represents the mountain of God as well as El Shaddai. What expression is most profound to you and why?

PRACTICE WRITING SHIN

♦ The letter SHIN (שׁ) is pronounced *sheen*. ♦

Start at the top right. Draw a slightly tilted line to your left until you hit the bottom line.

Then draw a straight line left and then up to the top left-hand corner for the letter.

Lift your pen to draw the center downward sloping line.

is the sound of the SHOFAR (שׁוֹפָר) that gathers all the broken pieces. It is the SHALOM (שָׁלוֹם) peace that breaks the authority of chaos and brings wholeness; and thus, ushers in the rest of the seventh day SHABBAT (שַׁבָּת) where the divine presence dwells —SHEKINAH (שְׁכִינָה).

WISDOM TWENTY-FOUR

ת
TAV

TAV (ת)

TAV (ת) is the twenty-second *Hebrew Living™ Letter* of the Alef-Bet whose pronunciation is *tav*. TAV (ת) has an ordinal value of 22 and a numerical value of 400, which means that the Hebrews can use it for either the number 22 or 400.

In ancient Hebrew, TAV (ת) means a sign. The picture of a sign is in the shape of a cross, or an "x" that marks the spot, which is seen in its ancient pictographs. The pictograph of the sign embodied in TAV (ת) symbolizes ownership, to seal, to make a covenant, to join two things together, and to make a sign. [81]

TAV (ת) IN ALEF-TAV (את)

You and I can personally choose to engage the essence of Messiah Yeshua—the Word of God—contained within the Hebrew letter TAV (ת). The seal of God's seal is the letter TAV (ת). It signifies faith, the conclusion, and the culmination of all 22 forces (letters) active in creation.

The Hebrew Word Picture for "religion"—*dat* (דת)—says that religion is the door of the sign, or the door of the cross:[82]

- DALET (ד)—door

- TAV (ת)—sign, covenant

The Hebrew Word Picture for "rest"—*Shabbat* (שבת)—tells us that we rest when we return to the covenant, or we return to the cross: [83]

- shoov (בש)—repent, return

- TAV (ת)—sign, covenant

The ALEF-TAV (את) redemption for TAV (ת) focuses on the sacrifice of Yeshua on the Cross for the redemption of the world.

---

[81] *Hebrew Word Pictures* by Frank T. Seekins, Tav, p. 96
[82] *Hebrew Word Pictures* by Frank T. Seekins, Religion, p. 98
[83] *Hebrew Word Pictures* by Frank T. Seekins, Sabbath - Rest, p. 98

Messiah Yeshua could have saved Himself. Instead, our incredible and loving Savior chose to lay down His own life for the salvation, deliverance, and redemption of the world.

> " *27 With Him they also crucified two robbers, one on His right and the other on His left. 28 So the Scripture was fulfilled which says, 'And He was numbered with the transgressors.' 29 And those who passed by blasphemed Him, wagging their heads and saying, 'Aha! You who destroy the temple and build it in three days, 30 save Yourself, and come down from the cross!' 31 Likewise the chief priests also, mocking among themselves with the scribes, said, 'He saved others; Himself He cannot save. 32 Let the Christ, the King of Israel, descend now from the cross, that we may see and believe.' 33 Now when the sixth hour had come, there was darkness over the whole land until the ninth hour. 34 And at the ninth hour Jesus cried out with a loud voice, saying, 'Eloi, Eloi, lama sabachthani?' which is translated, 'My God, My God, why have You forsaken Me?' 35 Some of those who stood by, when they heard that, said, 'Look, He is calling for Elijah!' 36 Then someone ran and filled a sponge full of sour wine, put it on a reed, and offered it to Him to drink, saying, 'Let Him alone; let us see if Elijah will come to take Him down.' 37 And Jesus cried out with a loud voice, and breathed His last. 38 Then the veil of the temple was torn in two from top to bottom. 39 So when the centurion, who stood opposite Him, saw that He cried out like this and breathed His last, he said, 'Truly this Man was the Son of God!' " (Mark 15:27-39).*

If you deny yourself, take up your cross, and follow Jesus, you will be humbled and be made of no reputation (Matt. 16:24-26; Mark 8:34; Luke 9:23).

> " *5 Let this mind be in you which was also in Christ Jesus, 6 who, being in the form of God, did not consider it robbery to be equal with God, 7 but made Himself of no reputation, taking the form of a bondservant, and coming in the likeness of men. 8 And being found in appearance as a man, He humbled Himself and became obedient to the point of death, even the death of the cross. 9 Therefore God also has highly exalted Him and given Him the name which is above every name, 10 that at the name of Jesus every knee should bow, of those in heaven, and of those on earth, and of those under the earth, 11 and that every tongue should confess that Jesus Christ is Lord, to the glory of God the Father"* (Philippians 2:5-11).

Thoughts

When Messiah Yeshua endured the cross for the joy set before Him, His eyes were on His Beautiful Bride.

" ¹ Therefore we also, since we are surrounded by so great a cloud of witnesses, let us lay aside every weight, and the sin which so easily ensnares us, and let us run with endurance the race that is set before us, ² looking unto Jesus, the author and finisher of our faith, who for the joy that was set before Him <u>endured the cross</u>, despising the shame, and has sat down at the right hand of the throne of God. ³ For consider Him who endured such hostility from sinners against Himself, lest you become weary and discouraged in your souls. ⁴ You have not yet resisted to bloodshed, striving against sin. ⁵ And you have forgotten the exhortation which speaks to you as to sons: 'My son, do not despise the chastening of the Lord, Nor be discouraged when you are rebuked by Him; ⁶ For whom the Lord loves He chastens, And scourges every son whom He receives.' ⁷ If you endure chastening, God deals with you as with sons; for what son is there whom a father does not chasten? ⁸ But if you are without chastening, of which all have become partakers, then you are illegitimate and not sons. ⁹ Furthermore, we have had human fathers who corrected us, and we paid them respect. Shall we not much more readily be in subjection to the Father of spirits and live? ¹⁰ For they indeed for a few days chastened us as seemed best to them, but He for our profit, that we may be partakers of His holiness. ¹¹ Now no chastening seems to be joyful for the present, but painful; nevertheless, afterward it yields the peaceable fruit of righteousness to those who have been trained by it" (Hebrews 12:1-11).

The last letter of *Hebrew Living™ Letters* —TAV (ת)—is also the last letter and seal of the word *emet* (אֱמֶת, truth). The three letters that spell *emet* are the beginning, middle, and ending letters of the Hebrew Alphabet: ALEF, MEM, TAV (אֱמֶת).

"Why are the letters of falsehood (שֶׁקֶר) consecutive in the Hebrew Alphabet while the letters of truth (אֱמֶת) are spread out?" "To indicate that falsehood is common, but the truth is uncommon." [84]

Truth is not only engraved on the Lord of the Universe's signet ring, it's also one of His Names.

"Jesus said to him, '<u>I am</u> the way, <u>the truth</u>, and the life. No one comes to the Father except through Me' " (John 14:6).

---

[84] *The Wisdom of the Hebrew Alphabet* by Michael L. Munk, p. 215

Thoughts

Truth is found the ALEF-TAV (את)'s Word.

> *"In the beginning was the Word, and the Word was with God, and the Word was God. . . . And the Word became flesh, and dwelt among us; and we saw His glory, glory as of the only Son from the Father, full of grace and <u>truth</u>" (John 1:1,14 _{NASB}).*

Christ's word warriors know the truth, and this is the truth that sets them free.

> *" ³¹ So Jesus was saying to those Jews who had believed Him, 'If you continue in My word, then you are truly My disciples; ³² and <u>you will know the truth, and the truth will set you free</u>' " (John 8:31-32 _{NASB}).*

We are sanctified in the truth and oneness of God's Word.

> *"¹⁷ <u>Sanctify them in the truth; Your word is truth</u>. ¹⁸ Just as You sent Me into the world, I also sent them into the world. ¹⁹ And for their sakes I sanctify Myself, so that they themselves also may be <u>sanctified in truth</u>. ²⁰ I am not asking on behalf of these alone, but also for those who believe in Me through their word, ²¹ that they may all be one; just as You, Father, are in Me and I in You, that they also may be in Us, so that the world may believe that You sent Me. ²² The glory which You have given Me I also have given to them, so that they may be one, just as We are one; ²³ I in them and You in Me, that they may be perfected in unity, so that the world may know that You sent Me, and You loved them, just as You loved Me. ²⁴ Father, I desire that they also, whom You have given Me, be with Me where I am, so that they may see My glory which You have given Me, for You loved Me before the foundation of the world" (John 17:17-24 _{NASB}).*

Thoughts

Redemption comes from the God of truth.

"¹ In You, Lord, I have taken refuge; Let me never be put to shame; In Your righteousness rescue me. ² Incline Your ear to me, rescue me quickly; Be a rock of strength for me, A stronghold to save me. ³ For You are my rock and my fortress; For the sake of Your name You will lead me and guide me. ⁴ You will pull me out of the net which they have secretly laid for me, For You are my strength. ⁵ Into Your hand I entrust my spirit; <u>You have redeemed me, Lord, God of truth</u>. ⁶ I hate those who devote themselves to worthless idols, But I trust in the Lord. ⁷ I will rejoice and be glad in Your faithfulness, Because You have seen my misery; You have known the troubles of my soul, ⁸ And You have not handed me over to the enemy; You have set my feet in a large place" (Psalms 31:1-8 _{NASB}).

Glory dwells in the land where graciousness and truth meet.

"⁴ Restore us, God of our salvation, And cause Your indignation toward us to cease. ⁵ Will You be angry with us forever? Will You prolong Your anger to all generations? ⁶ Will You not revive us again, So that Your people may rejoice in You? ⁷ Show us Your mercy, Lord, And grant us. Your salvation. ⁸ I will hear what God the Lord will say; For He will speak peace to His people, to His godly ones; And may they not turn back to foolishness. ⁹ Certainly His salvation is near to those who fear Him, <u>That glory may dwell in our land</u>. ¹⁰ <u>Graciousness and truth have met together</u>; Righteousness and peace have kissed each other. ¹¹ <u>Truth sprouts from the earth</u>, And righteousness looks down from heaven. ¹² Indeed, the Lord will give what is good, And our land will yield its produce. ¹³ Righteousness will go before Him And will make His footsteps into a way" (Psalms 85:4-13 _{NASB}).

Thoughts

The Way Of Wisdom

1. What is the significance that the three Hebrew letters that spell "truth" (אֱמֶת) covers the entire Hebrew Alphabet?

_____

_____

2. What does the Cross of Christ personally mean to you?

_____

_____

3. Dig for deeper riches involving the "cross" in Scripture. Read in context and meditate. In our TET (ט) chapter, you were led to research the "cross" in the Gospels. Now, cast your net for a wider search.

_____

_____

_____

"Looking unto Jesus, the author and finisher of our faith, who for the joy that was set before Him endured the **cross**, despising the shame, and has sat down at the right hand of the throne of God" (Heb. 12:2).

_____

_____

_____

"Having wiped out the handwriting of requirements that was against us, which was contrary to us. And He has taken it out of the way, having nailed it to the **cross**" (Col. 2:14).

_____

_____

_____

"For it pleased the Father that in Him all the fullness should dwell, [20] and by Him to reconcile all things to Himself, by Him, whether things on earth or things in heaven, having made peace through the blood of His **cross**" (Col. 1:19-20).

_____

_____

*"For many walk, of whom I have told you often, and now tell you even weeping, that they are the enemies of the **cross** of Christ: ¹⁹ whose end is destruction, whose god is their belly, and whose glory is in their shame—who set their mind on earthly things" (Phil. 3:18-19).*

_____

_____

_____

*"And being found in appearance as a man, He humbled Himself and became obedient to the point of death, even the death of the **cross**" (Phil. 2:8).*

_____

_____

*"And that He might reconcile them both to God in one body through the **cross**, thereby putting to death the enmity" (Eph. 2:16).*

_____

_____

*"But God forbid that I should boast except in the **cross** of our Lord Jesus Christ, by whom the world has been crucified to me, and I to the world" (Gal. 6:14).*

_____

_____

*"For the message of the **cross** is foolishness to those who are perishing, but to us who are being saved it is the power of God" (1 Cor. 1:18).*

_____

_____

4. The last letter of the ALEF-TAV's Alphabet—TAV (ת)—is also the last letter and seal of the word *emet* (אֱמֶת, truth). "Truth" is a vast topic in Scripture so let's initially narrow our search for "truth" to a single book in the Bible—the Book of Psalms—so we can learn from the man after God's own heart.

_____

_____

_____

*"He who walks uprightly, And works righteousness, And speaks the **truth** in his heart" (Psa. 15:2).*

_____

_____

_____

_____

*"Lead me in Your **truth** and teach me, For You are the God of my salvation; On You I wait all the day" (Psa. 25:5).*

_____

_____

_____

*"Into Your hand I commit my spirit; You have redeemed me, O L ORD God of **truth**" (Psa. 31:5).*

_____

_____

_____

*"For the word of the L ORD is right, And all His work is done in **truth**" (Psa. 33:4).*

_____

_____

_____

*"Do not withhold Your tender mercies from me, O L ORD; Let Your loving kindness and Your **truth** continually preserve me" (Psa. 40:11).*

_____

_____

_____

*"Behold, You desire **truth** in the inward parts, And in the hidden part You will make me to know wisdom" (Psa. 43:3).*

_____

_____

_____

*"Mercy and **truth** have met together; Righteousness and peace have kissed. **Truth** shall spring out of the earth, And righteousness shall look down from heaven"* (Psa. 85:10-11).

_____

_____

*"Teach me Your way, O Lord; I will walk in Your **truth**; Unite my heart to fear Your name"* (Psa. 86:11).

_____

_____

_____

_____

*"He shall cover you with His feathers, And under His wings you shall take refuge; His **truth** shall be your shield and buckler"* (Psa. 91:4).

_____

_____

_____

*"For Your mercy is great above the heavens, And Your **truth** reaches to the clouds"* (Psa. 108:4).

_____

_____

_____

*"The entirety of Your word is **truth**, And every one of Your righteous judgments endures forever"* (Psa. 119:60).

_____

_____

_____

*"The Lord is near to all who call upon Him, To all who call upon Him in **truth**"* (Psa. 145:18).

_____

_____

_____

TAV (ת)

What ALEF-TAV (את) riches of wisdom about the seal of TAV (ת) is most consequential for you and why?

PRACTICE WRITING TAV

● The letter TAV (ת) is pronounced *tav*. ●

Start at the top left drawing a RESH from the top left corner to the right bottom corner.

Then, move your pen slightly in from the upper left corner to draw a J-like line to the bottom line.

רכרכתתת   ①② ת

ת

ת

ת

ת

ת

ת

ת

ת

ת

is the name for a prayerful call to
God—TEFILA (תפילה).
TAV (ת) is the name for singing
God's praises through psalms—
TEHILIM (תְּהִלִּים). TAV (ת) is
the sound of returning to God
through repentance—
TESHUVAH (תְּשׁוּבָה), which
leads to the repairing of the
Universe—TIKKUN (תִּקּוּן)

BIBLIOGRAPHY

Bentorah, Chaim. *Learning God's Love Language*. Travelers Rest, South Carolina, True Potential, Inc., 2018.

Chumney, Edward. *The Seven Festivals of the Messiah*. Shippensburg, Pennsylvania: Treasure House (Destiny Image Publishers, Inc.), 2001.

Kushner, Lawrence. *The BOOK of LETTERS: A Mystical Alef-bet (Sefer Otiyot)*. Woodstock, Vermont: Jewish Lights Publishing, 15th Anniversary 2nd Edition, 1990.

Leitner, Dovid. *Understanding the ALEF-BEIS: Insights into the Hebrew Letters and Methods for Interpreting Them*. Nanuet, New York: Feldheim Publishers, 2007.

Merriam-Webster. *Merriam-Webster's Colligate Dictionary (10th Edition)*. Springfield, Massachusetts: Merriam-Webster Incorporated, 1993.

Mills, Dick and Michael, David. *Messiah and His Hebrew Alphabet*. Orange, California: Dick Mills Ministries, 1994.

Mitchell, David C. *The Songs of Ascents: Psalms 120 to 134 in the Worship of Jerusalem's Temples*. Newton-Mearns, Scotland UK: Campbell Publications, 2015.

Mozeson, Isaac E. *THE WORD: The Dictionary that Reveals the Hebrew Source of English*. New York, New York: SPI Books, 2000.

Munk, Rabbi Michael L. *The Wisdom in the Hebrew Alphabet*. Brooklyn, New York: Mesorah Publishing, Ltd., 1998.

Raskin, Rabbi Aaron L. *Letters of Light: A Mystical Journey Through the Hebrew Alphabet*. Brooklyn, New York: Rabbi Aaron L. Raskin and Sichos in English.

Seekins, Frank T. *Hebrew Word Pictures*. Phoenix, Arizona: Living Word Pictures, Inc., 2001.

Strong, James LL.D, S.T.D. *The New Strong's Exhaustive Concordance of the Bible*. Nashville, Tennessee: Thomas Nelson Publishers, 1995, 1996.

ABOUT THE AUTHOR

Robin Main is a prophetic artist, author, speaker, teacher and mentor who equips people to be the unique and beautiful creation that they have been created to be. She flows in love, revelation and wisdom with her SPECIALTY being kingdom enlightenment.

Her MISSION is to enlighten the nations by venturing to educate and restore the sons of the Living God.

Her CALL is a clarion one to mature sons, and the pure and spotless Bride of Christ who will indeed be without spot or wrinkle.

Her ULTIMATE DESIRE is that everyone be rooted and grounded in love, so they can truly know the height, width, breadth and depth of the Heavenly Father's love.

Reflections

Page #	Reflections

OTHER BOOKS BY ROBIN MAIN

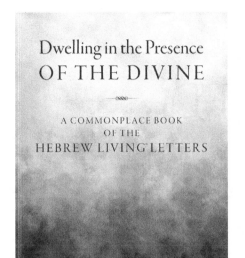

The Book of Creation is written in the language of the Hebrew Living™ Letters. When ALEF-TAV (את) built the House of Creation, it began with the quantum Hebrew letters of the Word of God. You are invited to discover for yourself the deepest energetic system of Creation, which God used as the building blocks for everything in heaven and earth. It is recommended that you start either with the *Dwelling in the Presence of the Divine: A Commonplace Book of the Hebrew Living™ Letters* or *ALEF-TAV's Hebrew Living™ Letters: 24 Wisdoms Deeper Kingdom Bible Study*; and then, advance to *Quantum 22™: The Hebrew Living™ Letters*. The ALEF-TAV Bible Study book serves as an on-ramp for the *Quantum 22™* Highway of Holiness. The *Dwelling in the Presence of the Divine: A Commonplace Book of the Hebrew Living™ Letters* is meant to be a companion to the Deeper Kingdom Bible Study— *ALEF-TAV's Hebrew Living™ Letters* and *Quantum 22™*; however, its presence-filled pages can be contemplated and savored all by themselves.

Additional books by Robin Main can be found at sapphirethroneministries.com

BLESSED

is the one who walks in the radiance
of ALEF-TAV (את)'s Presence.

Made in the USA
Las Vegas, NV
11 April 2024

88529274R00164